100 AMAZING FACTS ABOUT VOLCANOES

D1738273

Content

"In every volcano, there is a power that transcends human understanding."

— Jules Verne

Introduction

Hello, young explorer of the wonders of our planet! You hold in your hands "100 Amazing Facts About Volcanoes", a book that will take you on a fascinating journey through one of the most spectacular natural phenomena on Earth. Volcanoes, with their raw power and mysterious beauty, have captivated the human imagination for millennia. They are the creators of mountains, the sculptors of landscapes, and sometimes, the ruthless destroyers.

In this book, you're going to discover incredible stories and amazing facts about these smoking giants. You'll learn how they are born, why they erupt, and what secrets they hide beneath their bubbling surface. You'll be amazed by tales of molten lava, fly ash, and maybe even a little frightened by the devastating power of some historical eruptions. But don't worry, you're safe here, exploring these wonders from the pages of this book.

So, open your eyes wide, pique your curiosity, and get ready to be amazed. Your passion for nature, science and adventure is going to be fueled on every page. Let's go on an incredible journey into the fascinating world of volcanoes!

Marc Dresgui

Fact 1 - Birth of a Volcano

Do you know how a volcano is born? Think of the Earth as a big cake filled with very hot materials. Underneath the Earth's crust, there is magma, a burning mixture of molten rock and gas. When this magma rises to the surface, it creates a volcano. It's a bit like a bubble of hot syrup trying to pop out of a thick pancake.

It can take thousands of years for a volcano to originate. The magma slowly accumulates, forming a mountain. Sometimes it pierces the Earth's surface during an eruption, spewing lava, ash, and gases. These eruptions can be spectacular! Take the example of Paricutin in Mexico: in 1943, a cornfield turned into a 424-meter volcano in just one year.

A volcano can also be born underwater. These underwater volcanoes form mountains under the ocean. When they grow big enough, they emerge from the water, creating islands. The Hawaiian Islands were born this way, thanks to a chain of underwater volcanoes.

Each volcano has its own story. Some stay asleep for centuries before waking up, while others are constantly active. The birth of a volcano is a fascinating event that shows us the power and energy hidden beneath our feet.

Fact 2 - The Highest Volcano

Do you know the tallest volcano in the world? It is located in South America and is called the Ojos del Salado. This giant stands on the border between Argentina and Chile, reaching an impressive height of 6,893 meters. It's almost like stacking the Eiffel Tower seven times!

The Ojos del Salado is more than just a mountain. It is part of the Andes Mountains, a long mountain range that stretches along the west coast of South America. This region is known for its volcanic activity, as it is located on the Pacific Ring of Fire, an area where many volcanoes are active.

This volcano is not only tall, it is also very old. Scientists estimate that the Ojos del Salado was formed about a million years ago. Despite its great age, this volcano is still active. Its last eruption took place in the 20th century.

Although the Ojos del Salado is an extreme place, adventurers sometimes attempt to climb it. But be warned, this is a difficult and dangerous expedition! This volcano remains a testament to the power and natural beauty of our planet.

Fact 3 - Molten Lava

Have you ever seen molten lava? It is the incandescent material that erupts from volcanoes during an eruption. The lava is actually magma, which is molten rock, coming from the Earth's interior. When it reaches the surface, the magma is called lava. It can reach incredibly high temperatures, between 700 and 1,200 degrees Celsius!

The color of the lava can give you clues about its temperature. When very hot, it glows bright orange-red. As it cools, it turns dark red, then black. This transformation is fascinating to observe, but one should always keep a safe distance as lava is extremely dangerous.

Lava can create amazing shapes as it cools. For example, "basaltic organs" are columns of rock formed by the slow cooling of lava. You can see them in places like the Giant's Causeway in Northern Ireland. It's as if the lava were drawing giant sculptures!

Ultimately, molten lava is a powerful spectacle of nature. It builds and changes landscapes, creating new lands and shaping the world beneath our feet. Volcanoes and their lava are reminders of the dynamics and vibrancy of our planet.

Fact 4 - Volcanoes on Mars

Did you know that Mars, the Red Planet, is home to some of the largest volcanoes in our solar system? Unlike Earth, these Martian volcanoes have long since become extinct, but they remain wonders to explore. The most famous of these is Olympus Mons, the largest known volcano in the solar system.

The Olympus Mons is about 600 kilometers in diameter - that's almost as big as France! And how tall is it? It rises 22 kilometers above the Martian surface, making it almost three times higher than Everest. Imagine yourself standing on its summit, you'd be able to see a spectacular view of the Red Planet!

These volcanic giants tell us a lot about the history of Mars. Billions of years ago, Mars was geologically very active. Volcanic activity has played a key role in the formation of its landscape. It may even have created favorable conditions for life in the planet's distant past.

Martian volcanoes, although silent today, are witnesses to a tumultuous past. They remind us that Mars wasn't always the cold, barren world we see today. By studying these volcanoes, scientists hope to better understand the history of Mars and perhaps even that of our own planet.

Fact 5 - Mystery of the Crater

Have you ever heard of meteorite craters? Unlike volcanoes, these craters are not created by eruptions, but by the impact of meteorites hitting the Earth's surface. One of the most famous is the Barringer Crater in Arizona, USA. It is about 1.2 km wide and 170 meters deep, a true giant!

This crater was formed about 50,000 years ago, when a 50-meter-wide meteor of iron and nickel slammed into the Earth. The impact released energy equivalent to that of 20 million tons of TNT! It's as if thousands of bombs exploded at the same time, digging a huge hole in the ground.

Impact craters like Barringer's are important to scientists. They help to understand the forces that shape our planet and other celestial bodies. For example, the moon is covered with craters formed in the same way. Studying them can tell us a lot about space history.

The mysteries of the craters remind us how connected our planet is to space. Each crater is a window into Earth's distant past, a story written in stone and stars.

Fact 6 - Submarine Volcano

Did you know that volcanoes also exist under the sea? These underwater volcanoes are often hidden in the depths of the oceans. One of the most impressive is the Loihi, located near Hawaii. It is still active and continues to grow, slowly approaching the ocean's surface.

Submarine volcanoes form in the same way as those on land. Underneath the ocean, tectonic plates move and magma rises, creating a volcanic mountain. When these volcanoes erupt, they can expel lava and ash, but seawater quickly cools the lava, forming peculiar rocks and unique formations.

These volcanoes play a crucial role in the creation of new underwater ecosystems. For example, hydrothermal vents, formed by volcanic activity, are home to many forms of life, including some found nowhere else on Earth. These creatures adapt to living in extreme conditions, with little light and high temperatures.

Underwater volcanoes are therefore fascinating places, full of mysteries to be discovered. They show us how life can adapt and thrive even in the most inhospitable environments. By studying these volcanoes, scientists can learn more about the mysteries of the deep sea and the incredible diversity of life on our planet.

Fact 7 - Sleeping Giants

Have you ever heard of dormant volcanoes? These giants seem peaceful, but in reality, they are not extinct. They are simply dormant, able to wake up at any time. A fascinating example is Mount Fuji in Japan, a dormant volcano that hasn't erupted since 1707.

Dormant volcanoes have often become silent after periods of intense activity. Unlike extinct volcanoes, which should never erupt again, dormant volcanoes retain the ability to awaken. It can take centuries or even millennia, but magma can still rise to the surface and cause a new eruption.

Monitoring these volcanoes is essential. Scientists use instruments like seismographs to detect movements under the earth that could indicate an awakening. They also monitor gas emissions and changes in terrain formation around the volcano.

These sleeping giants remind us of the power hidden beneath the surface of our planet. Even though they are quiet now, their potential to erupt remains an important topic of study for scientists. By monitoring them, we can better understand how and when they might wake up, protecting people living nearby.

Fact 8 - Krakatoa Explosion

Do you know the story of the Krakatoa explosion? It is one of the most powerful volcanic eruptions ever recorded. In 1883, the Krakatoa volcano, located in Indonesia, erupted with terrifying force. This eruption has become famous all over the world for its immense power.

The explosion from Krakatoa was so loud that it was heard more than 3,000 kilometers away. Imagine the sound of an explosion so powerful it could be heard from so far away! Indeed, it is considered one of the largest sound explosions in Earth's recent history.

The eruption had dramatic consequences. It caused a gigantic tsunami, with waves up to 40 meters high. These waves devastated the surrounding coasts, causing the deaths of thousands of people. In addition, the eruption spewed a huge amount of ash and dust into the atmosphere, affecting the global climate.

The explosion of Krakatoa remains an important subject of study for scientists. It allows them to better understand the potential impacts of volcanic eruptions. This natural disaster shows the incredible strength of volcanoes and their ability to change the world around us.

Fact 9 - Volcanic Rocks

Have you ever held a volcanic rock in your hands? These rocks are formed by the cooling of lava. They are unique because they carry with them the history of volcanic eruptions. A famous example of volcanic rock is basalt, often found in lava flows.

Volcanic rocks are formed in different ways. If lava cools quickly in the open air, it forms rocks with small crystals, like basalt. But if it cools slowly underground, it forms rocks with large crystals, like granite. This difference can be clearly seen in the texture of the rocks.

These rocks are not only interesting to look at, they are also very useful. For example, basalt is often used in the construction of roads and buildings. Its strength and durability make it an ideal material for many applications.

Volcanic rocks tell us the secrets of the Earth's depths. Each rock has a fascinating history, revealing clues to the eruption that created it. Studying them helps us understand the geological processes that shape our planet.

Fact 10 - Islands Born of Fire

Did you know that some islands were created by volcanoes? That's right, many of the beautiful islands we know today are actually the result of underwater volcanic eruptions. Take the example of the Hawaiian Islands, one of the most famous island chains in the world, formed entirely by volcanic activity.

When an underwater volcano erupts, it expels lava, ash, and rocks. Over time, these materials accumulate, eventually forming an island above sea level. The process is slow and can take thousands or even millions of years.

Islands formed in this way often have unique characteristics due to their volcanic origin. For example, the island of Santorini in Greece is famous for its beautiful cliffs and spectacular landscape, shaped by multiple eruptions over the course of its history.

These "islands born of fire" are not only spectacular tourist destinations; They are also natural laboratories for scientists. By studying these islands, geologists can learn more about the formation of volcanoes and the evolution of the Earth. They are a reminder of the creative power of volcanoes and how they can shape our world.

Fact 11 - Lava Caves

Do you know lava caves? These incredible natural formations are created by the flow of lava. When a lava flow cools at the surface but remains fluid and hot underneath, it can form a tunnel. When the lava flows out of this tunnel, there is an empty cave: a lava cave.

These caves can be of all sizes, from small tunnels to vast caverns. One of the largest and most famous is the Thurston Lava Cave in Hawaii, which is part of Hawaii Volcanoes National Park. Visitors can walk through this tunnel formed about 500 years ago by a lava flow.

In addition to being spectacular, lava caves are important to science. They offer scientists a unique insight into the internal processes of a lava flow. By studying these caves, geologists can better understand the composition of lava and how it moves.

Lava caves are therefore natural wonders, witnesses to the powerful forces that shape our planet. They are a reminder of the dynamic activity beneath the Earth's surface and offer an extraordinary experience to those who explore them.

Fact 12 - Mount Vesuvius in Anger

Have you heard of Mount Vesuvius? It is one of the most famous volcanoes in the world, famous for its eruption in the year 79 AD. This eruption was so powerful that it completely covered and destroyed the Roman cities of Pompeii and Herculaneum.

Mount Vesuvius is located near Naples, Italy. Before the 79 eruption, it had been dormant for hundreds of years. People lived at his feet without suspecting the danger. But within hours, Mount Vesuvius spewed tons of ash and rocks, enveloping everything in a deadly cloud.

The eruption was so rapid and intense that the inhabitants of Pompeii and Herculaneum did not have time to flee. The ashes preserved their bodies in tragic poses, giving archaeologists a poignant glimpse into their final moments. Today, these cities are important archaeological sites, offering a unique look at ancient Roman life.

Mount Vesuvius remains one of the most closely watched volcanoes in the world. Although it has been quiet since its last eruption in 1944, it is still active and could wake up again. His story is a powerful reminder of the destructive force of volcanoes and the importance of watching over and respecting these sleeping giants.

Fact 13 - Volcanic Dust

Have you ever thought about the dust that comes out of volcanoes during an eruption? This dust, called volcanic ash, is very different from the ash from a wood fire. It is made up of tiny fragments of rock and glass, created when lava explodes in the air and cools rapidly.

This ash can travel very long distances. For example, during the 1980 eruption of Mount St. Helens in the United States, ash was transported thousands of miles. It covered cities and forests, altering landscapes in a matter of hours.

But volcanic ash isn't just about disorder and destruction. It plays an important role in soil fertilization. Rich in minerals, it can improve the quality of agricultural land, contributing to plant growth. This is one of nature's paradoxes: something so destructive can also help create life.

Volcanic dust therefore reminds us of the power of volcanoes and their ability to affect our world, from disrupting air travel to enriching soils. It is a witness to the dynamic forces at work beneath the Earth's surface.

Fact 14 - Volcanoes and Diamonds

Did you know that volcanoes play a role in the formation of diamonds? These gemstones do not form in the volcanoes themselves, but rather in the Earth's mantle, at depths of more than 150 kilometers. Diamonds rise to the surface thanks to very special volcanic eruptions.

These eruptions originate from volcanoes called "kimberlite pipes". When they erupt, they transport deep rocks, including diamonds, to the surface. The city of Kimberley, South Africa, is famous for these kimberlite pipes and has been a major site for diamond mining.

Diamonds formed in the Earth's mantle are made of pure carbon, subjected to extreme temperatures and pressures. It's this unique combination that makes them so hard and shiny. Without the activity of volcanoes, these diamonds would remain buried, out of our reach.

Diamonds from volcanoes are therefore a fascinating example of how deep geological processes affect our world on the surface. Each diamond is a small piece of Earth's history, brought to the surface by the power of volcanoes.

Fact 15 - The Sound of an Eruption

Have you ever imagined the sound a volcano makes when it erupts? It's an incredibly powerful and noisy phenomenon. When a volcano explodes, it can produce deafening noises, similar to bomb detonations or thunderclaps.

The intensity of the sound depends on the strength of the eruption. For example, the eruption of Krakatoa in 1883 was heard up to 4,800 kilometers away, in the Indian Ocean. It was so loud that people thought they could hear distant cannons. In fact, this eruption remains one of the loudest sounds ever recorded on Earth!

The sound of a volcanic eruption is not just noise. It carries with it important information for scientists. By analyzing these sounds, volcanologists can learn more about the strength of the eruption, the amount of material expelled, and even predict the future behavior of the volcano.

The sound of an eruption is therefore a powerful reminder of the power of nature. It reflects the energy released when a volcano erupts, offering a glimpse into one of our planet's most dynamic and impressive natural phenomena.

Fact 16 - Ice Volcanoes

Have you ever heard of ice volcanoes? Unlike ordinary volcanoes, ice volcanoes, or cryovolcanoes, eject water, ammonia, or methane instead of lava. These substances are usually in the form of ice or vapour. Cryovolcanoes are mostly found on the icy moons of giant planets and other objects in the outer solar system.

A famous example of cryovolcanism is on Enceladus, one of Saturn's moons. The jets of water vapor and ice ejected by Enceladus' cryovolcanoes are so powerful that they form one of Saturn's rings. It's an incredible sight to imagine!

Cryovolcanoes are important to scientists because they can provide clues to the presence of liquid water, a key ingredient for life, beneath the frozen surface of these moons. For example, Enceladus' geysers suggest that there is an ocean of liquid water beneath its icy surface.

These ice volcanoes are therefore fascinating phenomena that extend our understanding of volcanoes beyond Earth. They show us that even in the coldest and most remote environments, dynamic geological processes are at work.

Fact 17 - Volcanic Hot Water

Did you know that some volcanoes can create hot water? This hot water, also called "thermal", comes from the geothermal heat of volcanoes. When rainwater or water from rivers seeps into the ground and reaches hot rocks near volcanoes, it is heated and rises to the surface in the form of hot springs or geysers.

These hot springs are often found in active volcanic areas. For example, Iceland, known for its volcanic activity, is famous for its natural hot springs, such as the Blue Lagoon. These waters are not only relaxing for bathing, but can also be rich in health-promoting minerals.

In addition to creating hot springs, this heat can be used to produce geothermal energy. Geothermal power plants use steam from water heated by the earth to turn turbines and generate electricity. It is a renewable and clean source of energy.

Volcanic hot water is therefore a fascinating example of how the energy of a volcano can be used in a positive way. It not only provides a place for relaxation and healing, but also an environmentally friendly source of energy.

Fact 18 - Ash Cloud

You've probably heard of the ash clouds produced by volcanoes, haven't you? These clouds form when a volcano expels ash, small rock particles, and gases into the air during an eruption. These clouds can reach incredibly high altitudes and travel long distances.

An impressive example is the eruption of the Eyjafjallajökull volcano in Iceland in 2010. The ash cloud created by this eruption reached an altitude of 9 kilometers and disrupted air travel in Europe for several weeks. Thousands of flights were canceled, affecting millions of passengers.

Ash clouds aren't just a problem for airplanes. They can have a significant impact on human health and the environment. Ash particles are very fine and can cause respiratory problems when inhaled. In addition, ash can contaminate water, damage crops, and affect animal life.

However, ash clouds also have interesting effects on the climate. They can block sunlight, causing temperatures on the Earth's surface to drop temporarily. This phenomenon shows how volcanic eruptions can have a global impact on our planet.

Fact 19 - Magma in Motion

Do you know what happens beneath the Earth's surface before a volcanic eruption? It all starts with magma, a very hot liquid mixture of molten rock, gas, and minerals. This magma is constantly in motion, seeking a path through cracks and cavities beneath the earth.

Magma forms in the Earth's mantle, a layer just below the crust. As it heats up, it becomes less dense and begins to rise towards the surface. This process can take thousands of years. When magma reaches the surface, it becomes lava.

Sometimes, magma can create new cavities or paths as it moves. This can cause earthquakes and change the geological structure beneath the surface. Mount St. Helens, for example, experienced a series of earthquakes before its eruption in 1980, caused by the movement of magma.

Moving magma is therefore a key indicator for volcanologists. By monitoring these movements, they can often predict an impending eruption and warn local populations. Understanding the movement of magma is crucial to preventing disasters and protecting lives and property.

Fact 20 - Mud Volcanoes

Have you ever heard of mud volcanoes? These amazing phenomena don't spew lava, but mud! Mud volcanoes form when groundwater heated by geothermal deposits mixes with soil or rocks to create mud, which is then expelled to the surface.

These mud eruptions can be spectacular. For example, the Lusi mud volcano in Indonesia began erupting in 2006 and continued for several years, covering a large area and displacing thousands of people. Unlike traditional volcanoes, mud eruptions are generally slower and less violent.

Mud volcanoes are not only fascinating to observe, but they are also important for science. Scientists study these eruptions to learn more about underground geological processes. They can also provide information about the presence of natural gas and oil.

These unique volcanoes remind us of the diversity and complexity of our planet's geological phenomena. They show that volcanoes can manifest in unexpected ways, bringing ever more mysteries to be solved.

Fact 21 - Floating Pumice Stones

Have you ever seen a pumice? It is a type of volcanic rock that is very light and porous. What's so special about it? It can float on water! Pumice is formed when gas- and water-rich lava explodes violently, cooling quickly and trapping gas bubbles inside.

These stones are so light and porous because of the gas bubbles they contain. When lava cools rapidly, it solidifies before the gases have time to escape, creating a honeycomb structure. It is this structure that gives pumice its ability to float.

A fascinating example of this phenomenon was observed in 2012, when a huge raft of pumice, the size of nearly 400 football fields, was discovered floating in the Pacific Ocean. This raft was the result of an underwater eruption near New Zealand.

Pumice stones are useful for various applications. They are often used for polishing and exfoliation in the cosmetics industry, and can also be used in construction and gardening. Their lightweight and porous nature makes them versatile and valuable.

Fact 22 - Legends of Volcanoes

Did you know that many volcanoes are surrounded by fascinating legends? For centuries, cultures around the world have created stories to explain the eruption of volcanoes. These legends often reflect the fear and respect people have for these flaming mountains.

For example, in Hawaiian mythology, Goddess Pele is known as the goddess of volcanoes and fire. It is said that it inhabits the crater of the Kilauea volcano and that the eruptions are the result of its emotions. When Pele is angry, the volcano erupts.

In ancient Greece, the volcano on the island of Santorini was believed to be the abode of the giant Typhon, a terrifying monster that Zeus is said to have trapped under the mountain. The eruptions were believed to be attempts by Typhon to escape his prison.

These legends are not just old stories. They continue to influence the way people perceive and interact with volcanoes. In Iceland, for example, many locals still believe in spirits and elves inhabiting volcanoes and lava fields.

These mythological tales around volcanoes illustrate how natural phenomena can influence culture and beliefs.

Fact 23 - Smoking Fumaroles

Have you ever seen smoke coming out of the ground near a volcano? These fumes are called fumaroles. They are formed when volcanic gases, such as sulfur dioxide or carbon dioxide, escape from cracks in the earth's crust. These gases are often very hot and can give the impression that the ground is breathing.

Fumaroles are usually found in areas of high volcanic activity, where magma is close to the surface. They are a sign that the volcano is active, even if it does not erupt. For example, Yellowstone National Park in the United States is famous for its many fumaroles, a testament to the intense geothermal activity beneath the park.

These emanations are not only spectacular to observe, they are also important for scientists. By analyzing the gases emitted, volcanologists can learn a lot about the chemical composition of magma and the potential activity of the volcano.

Fumaroles are therefore fascinating and important phenomena. They remind us that the Earth is a living, active planet, with ever-changing processes beneath its surface. By observing them, we can better understand the power and complexity of volcanoes.

Fact 24 - Mount Etna Active

Do you know Mount Etna, one of the most active volcanoes in the world? Located on the island of Sicily, Italy, this giant rumbles and belches regularly, putting on an impressive show. Its constant activity has fascinated people since ancient times.

Mount Etna is a stratovolcano, which means it is composed of many layers of hardened lava and ash. This structure was formed over thousands of years of eruptions. Its eruptions are often accompanied by spectacular lava flows and sometimes even small earthquakes.

This volcano is not just a subject of study for scientists; It also has great cultural and historical significance. In Greek mythology, it was believed that the blacksmith of the gods, Hephaestus, had his forge under Mount Etna. The eruptions were seen as the result of his work.

Mount Etna is therefore more than just a volcano; It is a symbol of natural power and an important part of Sicilian cultural heritage. People come from all over the world to admire its eruptions and explore its slopes rich in history. Despite its dangerous nature, it remains a fascinating attraction and a source of wonder.

Fact 25 - Waterfalls of Fire

Have you ever heard of fire cascades? This rare and spectacular natural phenomenon occurs when lava from a volcano flows so fluidly and rapidly that it resembles a waterfall of liquid fire. It's an amazing vision of nature in action.

A famous example of this phenomenon can be seen in Hawaii Volcanoes National Park. Kilauea Volcano, one of the most active volcanoes in the world, sometimes has eruptions that create these incredible lava cascades. The glowing lava hurtles down the slopes of the volcano before plunging into the ocean, creating a stark contrast to the blue water.

These fire waterfalls are not only a magnificent sight, but they are also important for geologists. They make it possible to study the fluidity and composition of the lava, offering valuable clues to the underlying volcanic activity.

However, admiring these waterfalls of fire requires caution. Areas around volcanic eruptions can be dangerous due to toxic gases and intense heat. These waterfalls of fire are a powerful reminder of the beauty and power of our planet's natural forces.

Fact 26 - Seismography and Volcanoes

Do you know how scientists monitor volcano activity? One of the most important tools they use is the seismograph. These devices record earthquakes, which are often early signs of a volcanic eruption. Seismographs detect the smallest tremors, even those we can't feel.

When a volcano prepares to erupt, it produces earthquakes caused by the movement of magma beneath the surface. These tremors are called volcanic earthquakes. By measuring the frequency and intensity of these earthquakes, seismographs help scientists understand what's going on beneath the volcano.

A famous example of this monitoring is the eruption of Mount St. Helens in 1980. Prior to the eruption, seismographs recorded a significant increase in seismic activity, warning scientists that a major eruption was imminent. This information led to the evacuation of the area and the saving of many lives.

Seismographs are therefore essential tools for volcanologists. They make it possible to continuously monitor the seismic activity of volcanoes, offering crucial information for risk prevention and the protection of populations. Thanks to these devices, we can better understand and anticipate volcanic eruptions.

Fact 27 - Colors of Lava

Have you ever noticed that lava changes color? It's a fascinating phenomenon related to its temperature and composition. When lava is very hot, just after erupting from a volcano, it glows a bright orange-red. This is lava at its hottest, often over 1,000 degrees Celsius!

As the lava cools, its color changes. It goes from orange-red to dark red, then to brown and finally to black. This color change is due to the cooling of the minerals in the lava. For example, the black lava you often see is actually cooled and solidified lava.

The different colors of the lava give us clues about its temperature and fluidity. Orange-red lava is generally more fluid and flows more easily. In contrast, black lava, which is cooler, is often thicker and moves slowly.

So lava is not only an incredible natural spectacle, it is also an important scientific indicator. The colors of the lava help volcanologists understand the evolution of an eruption and predict the future behaviors of the volcano. It's a veritable palette of colors that tells us about the secrets of the Earth.

Fact 28 - Volcanic Winds

Have you ever heard of volcanic winds? These powerful winds are a fascinating phenomenon that occurs during volcanic eruptions. When a volcano erupts, it releases not only lava and ash, but also immense amounts of gas and water vapor. These emissions can generate very strong and hot winds around the volcano.

These volcanic winds are different from the usual weather winds. They are often laden with ash and particulate matter, and can be extremely hot, depending on how close the eruption is to the source. For example, during the eruption of Mount St. Helens in 1980, powerful winds were generated, blowing ash for hundreds of kilometers.

Volcanic winds can have a huge impact on the local environment. They can destroy vegetation, move ash and particles over great distances, and even affect the local climate temporarily. Their force can be destructive, toppling trees and damaging structures.

Scientists study these winds to better understand volcanic eruptions. By observing the direction and strength of the winds, they can learn more about the power of the eruption and the dispersion of ash and gases. This information is essential to assess the risks associated with eruptions and to help protect local communities.

Fact 29 - Volcanic Fertile Lands

Did you know that volcanic eruptions can create incredibly fertile land? It may seem surprising, but the ash and eruptive materials deposited by volcanoes are rich in essential nutrients for plants. This richness makes volcanic soils some of the most productive in the world.

Volcanic ash, while it can be destructive during an eruption, breaks down into soil rich in minerals like potassium, phosphorus, and calcium. These nutrients are vital for plant growth. For example, the Hawaiian Islands, with their native soil of lava and volcanic ash, are known for their extremely fertile soil.

This fertility is visible in agricultural regions located near active volcanoes. In Italy, for example, the areas surrounding Mount Etna are renowned for their vineyards and orchards. The volcanic soil provides a rich and unique environment for the cultivation of high-quality grapes.

However, growing on volcanic soils comes with risks. Farmers working near active volcanoes need to be prepared for the potential consequences of eruptions. Despite this, the richness of the volcanic soil makes it a valuable asset, often sought after for agriculture. Volcanic soils show how nature can transform a destructive event into a source of life and fertility.

Fact 30 - Volcano and Climate

Did you know that volcanoes can have a major impact on the Earth's climate? When a volcano erupts, it releases huge amounts of ash and gases into the atmosphere. These emissions can influence the climate on a global scale, sometimes significantly.

One of the gases emitted by volcanoes is sulfur dioxide. As it reaches the atmosphere, this gas can combine with water to form sulfate aerosols, which reflect sunlight. This can cause the Earth's surface to cool temporarily. For example, the eruption of Mount Pinatubo in the Philippines in 1991 resulted in a global cooling of about 0.5 degrees Celsius for several months.

However, this cooling effect is not the only impact of volcanic eruptions on the climate. Ash and aerosols can also disrupt precipitation patterns and reduce the amount of sunlight reaching the surface, affecting ecosystems and agriculture.

Scientists are studying these impacts to better understand the complex interactions between volcanoes and climate. This research helps predict the consequences of future eruptions and better prepare societies for these changes. Thus, volcanoes, although isolated natural phenomena, play an important role in the global climate dynamics of our planet.

Fact 31 - Unique Forms of Volcanoes

Did you know that not all volcanoes are the same? Indeed, they can take incredibly diverse forms, determined by the type of eruption and the composition of the lava. These different shapes make volcanoes fascinating geological structures.

Stratovolcanoes, for example, are characterized by their great heights and symmetrical conical shapes. They are formed by explosive eruptions that deposit alternating layers of lava, ash, and rock. Mount Fuji in Japan and Mount St. Helens in the United States are famous examples of stratovolcanoes.

At the other end of the spectrum, we have shield volcanoes. These volcanoes are usually very wide with gentle slopes. They are formed by eruptions of fluid lava that spread over great distances. Mauna Loa in Hawaii is a perfect example of a shield volcano.

There are also more unusual volcanoes, such as lava domes. These are mounds of viscous lava that accumulate around the volcano's opening. Mount Pelee in Martinique is an example of a lava dome.

Each type of volcano has its unique characteristics and offers a glimpse into the powerful forces at work beneath the surface of our planet. By studying these different forms, geologists can learn more about eruptive processes and volcanic activity.

Fact 32 - Lava Tube

Have you ever explored a lava tube? These incredible natural structures form when a lava flow on the surface cools and hardens, while the lava underneath continues to flow. When the lava flows completely, it leaves behind an empty tunnel. It's as if lava is digging its own path underground!

These tunnels can be of all sizes, with some large enough for a person to walk inside. They are like caves, with walls that are often smooth and undulating, testifying to the passage of lava. South Korea's Jeju Island, for example, is home to the Manjanggul Lava Tube, one of the longest lava tubes in the world.

Exploring a lava tube is a once-in-a-lifetime experience. It's like going back in time and seeing the traces left by an ancient lava flow. The walls of the tunnel can tell the story of the eruption that created it, revealing details about the temperature and velocity of the lava.

These tunnels are not only fascinating for tourists; They are also valuable to scientists. By studying them, geologists can learn more about the behavior of lava flows and the characteristics of volcanic eruptions. Lava tubes are therefore unique windows into the subterranean mysteries of volcanoes.

Fact 33 - Slag Cones

Do you know about slag cones? These small volcanic mountains are formed during relatively small eruptions. Slag cones are made up of fragments of volcanic rock, called slag, ejected by a volcano. These fragments accumulate around the eruptive mouth, forming a characteristic cone.

Slag is chunks of magma that have cooled rapidly in the air. They are usually small to medium in size and have a porous, lightweight texture. Scoria cones can vary in size, but are typically much smaller than stratovolcanoes or shield volcanoes.

A famous example of a cinder cone is the Paricutin in Mexico. This volcano is interesting because it appeared suddenly in a field in 1943 and grew rapidly, reaching about 424 meters in height in just 9 years. Its eruption has allowed scientists to study the birth and evolution of a volcano.

Slag cones are not only interesting for their formation; They also offer unique environments for flora and fauna. Over time, vegetation begins to grow on these cones, creating unique ecosystems. These volcanic structures are therefore valuable sources of information for geologists and biologists.

Fact 34 - Bubbling Geysers

Have you ever seen a geyser in action? These natural hot water fountains are a fascinating sight. Geysers form in areas of high geothermal activity, where groundwater is heated by the heat of magma. When the water gets hot enough, it turns to steam and bursts to the surface, creating a column of water and steam.

The process is a bit like a pot on the fire. The water in underground cavities is heated until it is hotter than its normal boiling point, due to the high pressure underground. When the pressure is released, the water quickly turns to steam, causing a dramatic eruption.

Yellowstone National Park in the United States is famous for its many geysers, including the famous Old Faithful. This geyser is particularly known for its regularity; It erupts almost every 90 minutes, attracting thousands of visitors each year.

Geysers are incredible natural phenomena that offer a glimpse of the power of geothermal energy. In addition to being tourist attractions, they are important for scientists studying geological and hydrological processes beneath the Earth's surface. These bubbling fountains are wonders of nature, a testament to the energy hidden beneath our feet.

Fact 35 - Extinct Volcanoes

Do you know what extinct volcanoes are? Unlike active or dormant volcanoes, extinct volcanoes are never expected to erupt again. They have been active in the past, but their activity has stopped, often because their source of magma has become depleted or blocked.

These extinct volcanoes can be identified by their absence of seismic or geothermal activity over a long period of time. For example, Mount Kilimanjaro in Tanzania is considered an extinct volcano. It has shown no signs of activity for millennia.

Even though extinct volcanoes no longer pose a threat of eruption, they remain important geological features. They can offer spectacular views and unique terrain for hiking and exploring. In addition, they are often of great cultural and historical importance to local communities.

Studying these extinct volcanoes helps scientists understand the life cycle of a volcano and the geological processes that lead to their formation and extinction. These silent giants are witnesses to the dynamic history of our planet, reminding us of the enormous forces that have shaped the Earth's surface over the ages.

Fact 36 - Mount Fuji, Sacred Mountain

Do you know Mount Fuji, Japan's iconic mountain? This magnificent volcano is not only famous for its natural beauty, but it is also considered a sacred place. At 3,776 meters, it is the highest peak in Japan and an important cultural symbol.

Mount Fuji is a stratovolcano, characterized by its near-perfect conical shape and explosive eruptions. Its last eruption was in 1707, but it is currently considered an active volcano. Its majestic presence can be seen from many places, including Tokyo on a clear day.

In Japanese culture, Mount Fuji has great spiritual significance. It has been a place of pilgrimage for centuries, attracting people in search of spiritual reflection and purification. Numerous works of art, including prints and paintings, depict it, testifying to its cultural and aesthetic significance.

Mount Fuji is therefore much more than just a volcano. It represents a union between nature, culture and spirituality, captivating visitors from all over the world. Its status as a sacred mountain reflects the way in which a natural phenomenon can acquire deep cultural and spiritual significance.

Fact 37 - Bright Eruptions

Have you ever seen images of volcanic eruptions lighting up the night sky? These luminous eruptions are not only spectacular, but they also reveal the power of natural forces at work. When a volcano erupts, it expels lava, ash, and gases, often creating an impressive light effect.

This phenomenon is particularly noticeable at night. The glowing lava, with its glowing orange hues, contrasts sharply with the surrounding darkness. In addition, eruptions can generate volcanic lightning, electrical discharges caused by the collisions of particles in the eruptive plume.

A notable example of this phenomenon is the eruption of the Eyjafjallajökull volcano in Iceland in 2010. Images of this eruption showed a spectacularly illuminated night sky, with lightning making its way through the columns of ash. It was both beautiful and intimidating.

These flares are not just a sight to behold; They also provide research opportunities for scientists. The study of these eruptions helps to better understand the internal processes of volcanoes and their impact on the atmosphere. Thus, each flare of light is a window into the dynamic forces that shape our planet.

Fact 38 - Mysterious Volcanic Island

Have you ever heard of the formation of a mysterious volcanic island? This happens when underwater volcanoes erupt and lava accumulates enough to emerge above the ocean's surface. These ephemeral islands can appear suddenly and sometimes disappear just as quickly, engulfed by erosion and ocean movements.

A recent example is the island of Nishinoshima, Japan. This island began to form in 2013 as a result of an underwater eruption. With successive eruptions, the island has continued to grow, attracting the attention of scientists and geologists around the world.

These new volcanic islands are of great scientific interest because they offer a unique opportunity to study how life begins to colonize new lands. Scientists are observing how plants and animals arrive on these islands and how ecosystems begin to develop.

The appearance of a mysterious volcanic island is a fascinating reminder of the dynamic nature of our planet. It shows how the Earth is constantly being reshaped by geological forces, creating new lands and shaping the oceans of our world.

Fact 39 - Volcanoes and Myths

Do you know the stories and legends related to volcanoes? Throughout history, many cultures have created myths to explain volcanic eruptions. These mythological tales often reflect people's fears and respect for the power and mysterious nature of volcanoes.

In Greek mythology, for example, it was believed that the god of fire, Hephaestus, had his forge under Mount Etna in Sicily. The eruptions were believed to be the result of his blacksmithing work. In Iceland, volcanoes were often linked to trolls or giants, powerful creatures from Norse mythology.

These myths were not only used to explain natural phenomena. They also had a social and cultural function, helping communities understand and manage the fear and uncertainty associated with eruptions. They were a way to make sense of events that were often devastating and unpredictable.

Today, although we understand the scientific causes of volcanic eruptions, these ancient myths and legends remain an important part of our cultural heritage. They remind us of how humans have always sought to make sense of the world around them, weaving stories and legends around the powerful forces of nature.

Fact 40 - Ash Floors

Did you know that volcanic ash can transform soils? When a volcano erupts, it expels large amounts of ash. These ashes, once they fall to the ground, can have a significant impact on the environment and agriculture.

Volcanic ash is rich in minerals such as silicon, calcium, and magnesium. When mixed with the soil, they can improve its fertility. This means that, despite the initial destruction caused by an eruption, farmland can sometimes benefit from these long-term mineral inputs.

However, in large quantities, ash can also be problematic. They can cover fields and smother crops. In addition, when wet, the ashes can form a thick, heavy mud that is difficult to remove. These aspects show the contrasting effects of volcanic ash on agriculture.

Throughout history, several civilizations have thrived on lands enriched by volcanic ash. The soils around volcanoes like Mount Vesuvius in Italy are among the most fertile in the world, thanks to past eruptions. These ash soils are a reminder of the lasting influence of volcanoes on our ecosystems and societies.

Fact 41 - Volcanic Acid Rain

Did you know that volcanic eruptions can cause acid rain? When a volcano erupts, it releases large amounts of gases, including sulfur dioxide, into the atmosphere. This gas can react with water in the atmosphere to form sulfuric acid, which then falls back down as acid rain.

This acid rain can have a big impact on the environment. It can damage forests, lakes, rivers and even buildings. Aquatic plants and animals are particularly vulnerable to acidity, which can alter the chemical balance of their habitat.

A notable example of this phenomenon is the eruption of Mount Pinatubo in the Philippines in 1991. This eruption produced massive amounts of sulfur dioxide, resulting in acid rain in the area. These rains have caused considerable environmental and agricultural damage.

However, acid rain is not just a negative phenomenon. They can also play a role in the natural regulation of ecosystems by eliminating certain invasive species or providing essential nutrients in certain environments. Scientists are studying these impacts to better understand and manage the consequences of volcanic eruptions on our environment.

Fact 42 - Volcanic Gases

Have you ever thought about the gases released by volcanoes during an eruption? These volcanic gases play a key role in eruptive processes and can have a significant impact on the environment. Volcanoes emit a variety of gases, such as sulfur dioxide, carbon dioxide, and water vapor.

Sulfur dioxide is one of the main gases produced by volcanoes. It can have significant effects on air quality and human health. When released into the atmosphere, it can form sulfate aerosols that impact the climate, helping to cool the Earth by reflecting sunlight.

Carbon dioxide, another volcanic gas, is a greenhouse gas. Although volcanoes release a relatively small amount of carbon dioxide compared to human emissions, it is important to monitor these emissions to understand their impact on climate change.

These volcanic gases are not only important for understanding eruptions. They also play a role in regulating the Earth's atmosphere over the long term. Scientists study these gases to better understand the interactions between geological processes and the atmosphere. Thus, volcanic gases are essential for grasping the complexity of our planet's natural systems.

Fact 43 - Smoke Plumes

Have you ever seen the towering plumes of smoke rising from an erupting volcano? These plumes, or eruptive columns, are an impressive mixture of gas, ash, and sometimes rock fragments. They can climb very high in the sky, sometimes up to several kilometers.

These plumes form when the pressure of molten magma and gases accumulated below the surface becomes too great. When the volcano erupts, these materials are forcefully expelled into the atmosphere. The type and amount of material ejected, as well as the strength of the eruption, determine the height and shape of the plume.

One of the most spectacular examples was the eruption of Mount St. Helens in 1980. Its ash plume rose more than 15 kilometers into the atmosphere, disrupting air traffic and blanketing surrounding areas with a layer of ash.

The plumes of smoke are not only a striking sight; They are also studied by scientists to better understand volcanic eruptions. Their characteristics can provide valuable information about the dynamics of the eruption and the associated risks. Thus, these eruptive columns are key indicators of volcanic activity and its potential impact on the environment.

Fact 44 - Acid Pools

Do you know about the acid pools associated with certain volcanoes? These basins are extremely acidic bodies of water, formed in or near volcanic craters. Their acidity comes from volcanic gases like sulfur dioxide that dissolve in water, creating acidic solutions such as sulfuric acid.

These pools often have bright and dramatic colors, ranging from yellow to emerald green, due to the presence of dissolved minerals. However, their beauty hides a danger: their acidity is such that it can dissolve metals and burn human skin. The crater lake of the Kawah Ijen volcano in Indonesia is a famous example, known for its blue flames and acidic lake.

Acid pools are important to scientists because they allow the interactions between water and volcanic gases to be studied. They provide clues about the chemical processes that occur beneath the Earth's surface and can help understand the risks associated with volcanic activity.

These acid pools, despite their hostility, are fascinating ecosystems. They show the ability of life to adapt to the most extreme environments, with some microorganisms being able to survive and even thrive in these acidic conditions. These extreme environments therefore offer unique windows into the resilience of life and the chemical dynamics of volcanic systems.

Fact 45 - Gas Explosions

Have you ever heard of gas explosions in volcanoes? These explosions occur when gases trapped in magma are released suddenly and violently. These gases, often under high pressure beneath the Earth's surface, can cause dramatic eruptions when they escape.

The process begins when magma rises to the surface. As it gets closer, the pressure decreases, allowing dissolved gases to escape. If a lot of gas is released quickly, it can lead to an explosion. The intensity of the explosion depends on the amount of gas, the rate at which it is released, and the viscosity of the magma.

A dramatic example of this phenomenon is the eruption of Mount St. Helens in 1980. A huge side explosion was triggered by the rapid release of pressurized gases, destroying much of the volcano's summit and sending an ash plume miles into the sky.

These gas explosions are an important aspect of the study of volcanoes. Scientists monitor them to understand the underlying mechanisms of volcanic eruptions and to assess the associated risks. Understanding how and why these explosions occur can help predict future eruptions and protect communities near volcanoes.

Fact 46 - Volcanic Minerals

Have you ever thought about the origin of minerals in volcanic rocks? Volcanoes play an essential role in the formation of many minerals. When a volcano erupts, it expels lava which, as it cools, forms rocks containing various minerals. These minerals are created by the crystallization of magma.

These volcanic rocks, such as basalt and andesite, are often rich in minerals such as olivine, feldspar, and quartz. Their composition varies depending on the chemical composition of the original magma. For example, basalt, which is derived from low-viscosity lava, typically contains minerals like olivine and pyroxene.

These minerals are not only important for geology; They also have practical applications. Some, such as quartz, are used in the construction industry and for jewelry making. Others, such as olivine, can be used in industrial processes or as abrasives.

Volcanic minerals are therefore a valuable source of materials for different industries. They offer a fascinating insight into the natural processes that take place beneath the Earth's surface and are a reminder of the influence volcanoes have on our world.

Fact 47 - Fiery Clouds

Have you ever heard of the fiery clouds? These incredibly dangerous phenomena are avalanches of hot gases, ash, and rocks that descend the slopes of a volcano during an eruption. They can reach incredibly high speeds, up to 700 kilometers per hour, and temperatures exceeding 1,000 degrees Celsius.

Fiery clouds are generated by the collapse of an eruptive column or by the explosion of a lava dome. These clouds of incandescent material are so dense and hot that they follow the relief of the ground, destroying almost everything in their path. Their high speed and temperature make them particularly deadly.

A tragic example of the power of the fiery clouds was the eruption of Mount Pelée in Martinique in 1902. A fiery cloud rolled down the mountain and destroyed the town of St. Peter in a matter of minutes, killing an estimated 30,000 people. This event highlighted the need for better understanding and monitoring of volcanoes.

Fiery clouds are therefore critical aspects of some volcanic eruptions. Their study helps scientists better understand and predict the behaviour of volcanoes, with the aim of reducing risks to people living nearby. These phenomena demonstrate the destructive power of volcanoes and the need to respect these giants of nature.

Fact 48 - Effusive Eruptions

Have you ever heard of effusive eruptions? Unlike explosive eruptions that spew ash and rocks into the air, effusive eruptions are characterized by the slow and steady flow of lava. These eruptions typically produce lava flows rather than ash clouds or fiery clouds.

This type of eruption is typical of shield volcanoes, such as those found in Hawaii. The lava emitted is usually very fluid, allowing it to flow easily over large distances. For example, Mauna Loa, one of the most active volcanoes in the world, is known for its long, wide lava flows.

Although effusive eruptions are less spectacular than explosive eruptions, they can still be dangerous. Lava flows can destroy homes, roads and alter landscapes. However, they often offer more time for evacuation and precautionary measures.

Effusive eruptions are important to scientists because they provide information about the composition of magma and the internal processes of volcanoes. Studying these eruptions helps to understand how volcanoes shape our planet over time. These lava flows are a testament to the dynamic and constantly changing nature of the Earth.

Fact 49 - Cone Formation

Do you know how volcanic cones are formed? These iconic structures are the result of the accumulation of material ejected by a volcano during an eruption. Each eruption can deposit lava, ash, rocks, and slag, which pile up around the crater to form a cone.

The cones can vary greatly in size and shape, depending on the type of eruption and the material being ejected. Ash cones, for example, are usually formed by explosive eruptions that spew small particles into the air. These particles then fall back around the eruptive vent, forming a cone with relatively gentle slopes.

Slag cones, on the other hand, form from larger fragments of volcanic rock. These fragments, called slag, are ejected into the air and fall back near the eruptive vent, forming cones with steeper slopes. A famous example of a cinder cone is the Paricutin in Mexico, which was born in a cornfield in 1943.

The formation of these cones is a fascinating process that shows the power of volcanic eruptions. Each layer of ejected material tells the story of a particular eruption, offering scientists valuable clues about the volcano's past activity. Thus, volcanic cones are not only impressive geological features; They are also natural archives of volcanic activity.

Fact 50 - Animals of the Volcanoes

Have you ever thought about animal life around volcanoes? Despite harsh conditions, many animals have adapted their lives around these giants of nature. Volcanic ecosystems, often isolated and unique, are home to astonishing biodiversity, including endemic species found nowhere else on Earth.

In volcanic regions, you can find a variety of animals that have developed special adaptations to survive. For example, on the Galapagos Islands, formed by volcanoes, live unique species such as the famous giant tortoises and marine iguanas. These animals have adapted to thrive in an environment influenced by volcanic activity.

Active volcanoes, such as those in Hawaii, also provide nutrient-rich habitats thanks to the fertile soils created by volcanic eruptions. This fertility promotes the growth of abundant plants, supporting a diverse food chain, from insects to birds.

The animals of volcanoes show us the resilience of life in the face of challenges. Their ability to adapt and thrive in such dynamic environments is a fascinating testament to the diversity of life on our planet. These volcanic ecosystems are natural laboratories for studying the adaptation and evolution of species.

Fact 51 - Silent Volcanoes

Do you know what silent volcanoes are? Unlike active or dormant volcanoes, silent volcanoes show no signs of activity. They have no eruptions, earthquakes or gas emissions. However, this does not necessarily mean that they are extinguished; They may simply be in a prolonged quiet phase.

These volcanoes can remain silent for centuries or even millennia. During this time, it may seem that they have become an inert part of the landscape. But beneath the surface, geological processes continue. Magma may still be present, simply waiting for the right conditions to manifest again.

An example of a silent volcano is Mauna Kea in Hawaii. Although it is classified as an active volcano, its last eruption was around 4,500 years ago. Today, it is best known for its astronomical observatories, taking advantage of its high peak and clear skies.

Silent volcanoes are important to scientists because they represent a geological mystery. Their study helps understand the life cycles of volcanoes and can provide clues to future eruptions. Thus, even in their silence, these volcanoes offer valuable information about the internal dynamics of our planet.

Fact 52 - Crystals in Lava

Have you ever noticed shiny crystals in a volcanic rock? These crystals form in lava as it cools and hardens. Lava is a mixture of molten rocks and minerals that, as it cools, form crystals of different sizes and shapes.

The size and type of crystal depends on several factors, such as the rate at which the lava cools and its chemical composition. For example, slow cooling allows large crystals to form, while rapid cooling results in the formation of small crystals or almost entirely glassy rock with no visible crystals.

Some of the most common crystallized minerals in lava are olivine, feldspar, and quartz. These minerals give volcanic rocks their unique texture and color. For example, olivine, a green mineral, can be found in some basaltic lavas, giving it a characteristic green color.

These crystals are not only beautiful; They are also important for geologists. By studying these crystals, scientists can learn more about the conditions under which the lava cooled and the history of volcanic activity. Thus, the crystals in the lava are like little clues about the internal processes of volcanoes.

Fact 53 - Underground Heat

Have you ever thought about all the warmth under our feet? The Earth is incredibly hot at depth, and this subsurface heat is closely linked to volcanic activity. The Earth's internal heat, or geothermal energy, is largely due to the radioactive decomposition of minerals and the flow of heat from the Earth's core.

This subsurface heat plays a crucial role in the formation of magmas, which are the cause of volcanic eruptions. When the rock in the Earth's mantle is heated, it begins to melt, forming magma. This magma can then rise to the surface, resulting in volcanic eruptions.

In some parts of the world, this geothermal heat is harnessed as an energy source. Geothermal power plants use steam produced by underground heat to turn turbines and generate electricity. Iceland, for example, gets much of its energy from geothermal resources.

Subsurface heat is therefore an essential part of our planet, influencing both geological processes and our use of energy resources. It is a reminder of the dynamics and power of the Earth, continually shaping the world on its surface.

Fact 54 - Lost Islands

Have you ever heard of islands created by volcanoes and then disappeared? These ephemeral islands appear when an underwater volcano erupts, throwing enough material to the surface to form an island. However, these islands are not always meant to last. Often, they are eroded by waves or collapse under their own weight.

A famous example is the island of Surtsey, born in 1963 near Iceland following an underwater eruption. Initially, the island measured about 2.7 km², but erosion has reduced its size over the years. Although Surtsey has survived to the present day, many other similar volcanic islands disappeared shortly after their formation.

These temporary islands are of interest to scientists because they offer a unique opportunity to study the early stages of ecological evolution. For example, Surtsey has been closely monitored to see how life colonizes new lands.

The birth and disappearance of these islands show the dynamic nature of our planet. They remind us that the Earth is constantly evolving, shaped by the powerful forces of geology and oceanography. These ephemeral islands are testaments to nature's astonishing ability to create and transform landscapes.

Fact 55 - Volcanoes of yesteryear

Have you ever thought about what volcanoes might have been like in our planet's distant past? The volcanoes of old, which shaped the Earth millions of years ago, played a crucial role in shaping our current environment. These ancient volcanoes not only created new land, but also had a significant impact on the climate and the evolution of life.

For example, about 250 million years ago, massive eruptions in the Siberian region, known as the Siberian Trapps, released huge amounts of gas into the atmosphere. These eruptions are thought to have contributed to one of the largest mass extinctions in Earth's history, the end of the Permian.

These ancient volcanoes also played a role in the creation of rich deposits of minerals and rocks. Igneous and metamorphic rocks formed from volcanic activity are the source of many valuable mineral deposits and spectacular geological formations.

Studying these ancient volcanoes helps geologists understand the Earth's geological history. They can reconstruct past events and see how volcanic activity has influenced the evolution of our planet. These ancient volcanoes are windows into Earth's dynamic past, revealing the secrets of its long and fascinating history.

Fact 56 - Synchronized Eruptions

Have you ever heard of synchronized volcano eruptions? It is a rare and fascinating phenomenon where several volcanoes erupt almost simultaneously or in a very short period of time. Although synchronized eruptions may appear to be coordinated, they are often the result of independent geological processes coinciding by chance.

Synchronized eruptions can occur in areas where multiple volcanoes are geographically close and share a common source of magma. However, in some cases, synchronized eruptions occur between volcanoes that are not physically linked, suggesting more complex influences such as changes in regional tectonic constraints.

A historical example of this phenomenon is the simultaneous eruption of several volcanoes along the Lesser Antilles arc in 1902. This series of eruptions, including that of Mount Pelée in Martinique and Soufriere in St. Vincent, coincided in time, although the volcanoes are not directly related.

These synchronized eruptions are of particular interest to volcanologists because they can offer clues to the underlying geological processes affecting a large region. Studying these events can help to better understand the interactions between volcanoes, tectonic plates, and magma systems.

Fact 57 - Growing Mountains

Have you ever thought that some mountains are actually volcanoes that are growing? Every time a volcano erupts, it expels lava, ash, and rocks that, as they accumulate, can increase the size of the volcano. Over time, these successive eruptions can transform a small volcanic cone into a towering mountain.

This growth process is particularly evident in active volcanoes that experience frequent eruptions. For example, Mount St. Helens in the United States has significantly changed in shape and size as a result of its successive eruptions, especially the major eruption of 1980.

Eruptions don't just contribute to the vertical growth of a volcano; they can also change the structure and scope of the process. The build-up of lava and ash can expand the base of the volcano, creating a wider, more imposing profile.

These growing mountains are a fascinating reminder of the dynamic nature of volcanoes. They illustrate the power of the Earth to reshape and evolve. Growing volcanoes provide a valuable opportunity for scientists to study geological processes in action and understand how our planet's landscapes have formed over time.

Fact 58 - Lava Fields

Have you ever explored a lava field? These impressive expanses are the result of effusive eruptions, where lava flows slowly and spreads over large areas before cooling and hardening. These lava fields can vary in size, ranging from a few square meters to several square kilometers.

The texture and appearance of a lava field depends on the nature of the lava. For example, pāhoehoe lava, typical of Hawaiian volcanoes, creates fields with smooth, undulating surfaces. In contrast, ʻaʻā lava forms rough, choppy fields, with sharp, unstable chunks of rock.

These lava fields provide a unique landscape for exploration and study. Scientists can learn a lot about the history of an eruption and the characteristics of magma by studying these fields. Lava formations also provide habitats for a variety of plants and animals, which adapt to survive in these harsh environments.

Lava fields are therefore fascinating witnesses to the power of volcanic eruptions. They illustrate nature's ability to transform landscapes and create new environments. Exploring these fields offers a unique experience and insight into the geological forces that shape our planet.

Fact 59 - Ash Hills

Have you ever seen hills formed entirely of volcanic ash? These hills, often referred to as cinder cones, form during explosive eruptions. During these eruptions, tons of ash and small fragments of rock are thrown into the air and fall around the volcano, gradually forming a hill or cone.

These cinder cones have a relatively simple structure and are generally smaller than large stratified volcanoes. Their shape is often symmetrical with steep slopes, resulting from the accumulation of ash around a central point. A famous example is the Sunset Crater in Arizona, which offers an impressive lunar landscape.

Although smaller than other types of volcanoes, cinder cones play an important role in the volcanic ecosystem. Over time, vegetation begins to grow on this ash, helping to stabilize the soil and create habitat for plants and animals.

These ash hills are therefore fascinating witnesses to volcanic activity and nature's ability to regenerate after destructive events. Their study helps scientists better understand explosive eruptions and their impacts on the environment. These unique natural formations also provide opportunities for exploration and education about our planet's geological processes.

Fact 60 - Crater Lakes

Have you ever admired the beauty of a crater lake? These lakes form in craters left behind by volcanic eruptions. After the activity of a volcano, the crater can fill with rainwater or groundwater, creating a lake. These crater lakes can vary greatly in size and depth.

One of the most famous examples is Crater Lake in Oregon, USA. Formed about 7,700 years ago following the collapse of the Mazama volcano, it is one of the deepest lakes in the world. Its deep blue color and clear waters make it a stunning natural spectacle.

These lakes are not only beautiful; they are also scientifically valuable. Crater lakes can give clues to past and current volcanic activity. Scientists study their chemistry, temperature, and water level to monitor changes in underlying volcanic activity.

Crater lakes are also unique ecosystems. They may be home to specialized plant and animal species, adapted to life in these particular environments. Thus, crater lakes offer a fascinating glimpse into the dynamics of nature, showing how life can thrive even in landscapes shaped by volcanic forces.

Fact 61 - Frozen Volcanoes

Have you ever heard of frozen volcanoes? These volcanoes, located in polar or high-altitude regions, present a stark contrast between the intense heat of their volcanic activity and the frigid environment that surrounds them. They are often covered in snow and ice, even when they are active.

One of the most fascinating aspects of frozen volcanoes is their ability to interact with the surrounding ice and snow. When they erupt, the heat from the lava can quickly melt the ice, creating mud and water flows called lahars. These lahars can be as devastating as the lava flows themselves.

A famous example is Mount Erebus in Antarctica, one of the few active volcanoes on this icy continent. Its presence is remarkable, with steam emanations rising above the ice and ice formations created by the volcanic gases emitted.

Frozen volcanoes are important to science because they offer unique insight into the interactions between volcanic geology and cold climates. Researchers are studying these volcanoes to understand how they influence their glacial environment and to better predict the risks associated with their activity. These volcanoes illustrate the incredible diversity of volcanic phenomena and nature's ability to adapt to extreme conditions.

Fact 62 - Magma in Depth

Do you know where the magma that fuels volcanic eruptions comes from? Magma is a mixture of molten rocks, gases, and crystals that forms deep within the Earth. It is usually found in the Earth's upper mantle and crust, where temperatures and pressures are high enough to melt rock.

The formation of magma is a complex process. It can occur in a variety of ways, such as the decompression of the mantle as one tectonic plate moves away from another, or the melting of the Earth's crust due to the heat of a plunging plate in a subduction zone. The type of magma produced varies according to its chemical composition, which in turn is influenced by the source rock and melting conditions.

This magma can remain below the surface for extended periods of time, forming magma chambers. When the pressure in these chambers becomes too great, or changes in the Earth's crust allow magma to escape, it rises to the surface and can lead to a volcanic eruption.

Scientists study magma in depth to better understand volcanic processes. By analyzing the composition of magma and monitoring movements below the surface, they can better predict eruptions and understand the internal dynamics of our planet.

Fact 63 - Eruptive Cycles

Have you ever heard of volcano eruptive cycles? An eruptive cycle refers to the periods of activity and rest that a volcano may experience over time. These cycles can vary greatly from volcano to volcano, ranging from a few years to several millennia.

Eruptive cycles are influenced by many factors, including the amount of magma available, changes in tectonic plate movements, and even water levels in the Earth's crust. Some volcanoes may have relatively regular cycles, while others have unpredictable and sporadic eruptions.

Understanding these cycles is crucial for volcanologists. By studying a volcano's past patterns of activity, scientists can better predict its future eruptions. This is particularly important for risk prevention in inhabited areas close to volcanoes.

The eruptive cycles of volcanoes remind us that the Earth is a dynamic and changing planet. They illustrate how the underlying geological forces shape the Earth's landscape over time, altering ecosystems and influencing human societies. These cycles are fascinating windows into the powerful and unpredictable nature of volcanoes.

Fact 64 - Volcanic Observatories

Have you ever visited or heard of a volcanic observatory? These centers are essential for the monitoring and study of volcanoes. They are equipped with advanced technologies to track volcanic activity, such as seismographs to detect earthquakes, sensors to measure gas emissions, and cameras to observe visual changes.

Volcano observatories play a crucial role in preventing volcano hazards. By continuously monitoring for signs of an impending eruption, such as an increase in seismic activity or changes in gas emissions, they can alert authorities and local populations, enabling timely evacuations and saving lives.

A famous example is the Hawaii Volcano Observatory, which monitors the archipelago's active volcanoes, including Kīlauea and Mauna Loa. Through their work, scientists have been able to provide valuable information and warnings during recent eruptions.

Volcanic observatories are not just monitoring centers; They are also places of scientific research. Researchers study volcanic processes there to better understand how volcanoes function, which helps improve methods for monitoring and predicting eruptions. These observatories are therefore essential pillars in the management of volcanic risks and in the advancement of volcanological science.

Fact 65 - Super Volcanoes

Have you ever heard of super volcanoes? These giants of Earth are capable of such massive eruptions that they can have a global impact. A super volcano differs from ordinary volcanoes in the enormous amount of magma it can eject. These eruptions can throw thousands of cubic kilometers of material into the atmosphere.

One of the most worrisome aspects of super volcanoes is their potential to cause "volcanic winters." Major eruptions can inject large amounts of ash and sulfur gas into the atmosphere, blocking sunlight and lowering global temperatures. This can lead to drastic climate changes and affect life on Earth.

A famous example of a super volcano is Yellowstone National Park in the United States. Although it hasn't had a major eruption in thousands of years, its huge underlying magma chamber is a testament to its explosive potential.

Despite their name and destructive potential, super volcanoes are not a daily threat. Their eruption is an extremely rare event. Scientists are studying them carefully to better understand their eruptive cycles and the warning signs of a possible eruption. Thus, super volcanoes, while a source of fascination and awe, are also crucial subjects of study for understanding large-scale geological processes.

Fact 66 - Expanding Islands

Did you know that some islands are constantly expanding due to volcanic activity? These islands, formed by underwater volcanic eruptions, can grow over time as new eruptions add more lava, ash, and other volcanic material. This natural process continually changes their size and shape.

An impressive example of this phenomenon is the island of Surtsey, located near Iceland. Born from an underwater eruption in 1963, it continued to expand with new eruptions for several years. Although erosion has since reduced in size, the island continues to be a site of interest for scientists studying the evolution of ecosystems.

These expanding islands are natural laboratories for the study of biology, geology, and ecology. Scientists can observe how life colonizes new lands and how ecosystems develop from scratch.

In addition to providing a field of study for scientists, these islands bear witness to the power and dynamics of our planet's geological processes. They remind us that the Earth's surface is constantly changing, shaped by the powerful forces of nature. These expanding islands are fascinating examples of Earth's ability to create new lands.

Fact 67 - Volcanic Gemstones

Did you know that some of the most beautiful jewels come from the depths of volcanoes? Volcanic gemstones, such as diamonds, rubies, and sapphires, form under extreme conditions of temperature and pressure associated with volcanic activity. These conditions favor the creation of unique and beautiful crystals.

Diamonds, for example, form in the Earth's mantle and are transported to the surface by deep volcanic eruptions. These eruptions form rocks called kimberlites, which often contain diamonds. It is by extracting these rocks that the diamonds are recovered.

Sapphires and rubies also form under conditions of high pressure and temperature. They are often found in volcanic ash deposits or lava flows. The variety of colors of these gems comes from the traces of different chemical elements present during their formation.

These gemstones are not only aesthetically admirable, but they are also scientifically significant. They provide clues to the geological processes that take place beneath the Earth's surface. Thus, volcanic gemstones are treasures of nature, testifying to the beauty that can emerge from the most tumultuous forces of our planet.

Fact 68 - Clarity After Ashes

Have you ever noticed how quickly nature can regenerate after a volcanic eruption? Despite the initial destruction caused by ash and lava flows, the ecosystem often recovers with surprising vigour. This phenomenon, which could be called "clarity after ashes", shows the resilience of nature.

After an eruption, layers of volcanic ash can actually enrich the soil with nutrients, helping to stimulate plant growth. Once the ash mixes with the soil, it provides essential minerals that can improve soil fertility. As a result, there is often a rapid resurgence of vegetation.

In addition to enriching soils, volcanic eruptions can also alter landscapes, creating new ecological niches. These changes may lead to the emergence of new species or the migration of existing species to these new areas.

Thus, volcanic eruptions, while destructive in the short term, can lead to increased ecological diversity and productivity in the long term. This ability of nature to recover and thrive after major disruptions is a remarkable example of ecosystem dynamics and resilience.

Fact 69 - Lava Waves

Have you ever seen images of "lava waves"? This spectacular phenomenon occurs during effusive eruptions, where fluid lava flows like water. When this lava encounters obstacles or variations in terrain, it can form ripples or movements that resemble waves.

These lava waves are typical of pāhoehoe lava, which are particularly fluid and hot. This fluidity allows them to move quickly and cover large areas, sometimes forming wavy or curled patterns in their path. Their movement is hypnotic and can look surprisingly graceful, despite the extremely high temperatures.

One of the best places to observe this phenomenon is in Iceland or Hawaii, where volcanoes regularly produce this type of lava. Pāhoehoe lava flows are fascinating to watch, but they are also extremely dangerous due to their temperature and mobility.

Lava waves aren't just an impressive natural spectacle; They are also important for geological studies. They help scientists understand the dynamics of effusive eruptions and the nature of magma. This phenomenon illustrates the power and beauty of geological processes in action.

Fact 70 - Ash Deserts

Have you ever heard of the ash deserts created by volcanic eruptions? These unique landscapes form when large amounts of volcanic ash accumulate over vast areas, creating an environment that resembles a desert. These ash deserts can stretch for miles, covering the earth with a thick layer of fine particles.

The appearance of an ash desert is often the result of major explosive eruptions. During these eruptions, the volcano spews immense amounts of ash into the air, which then falls to the ground. A striking example is the eruption of Mount St. Helens in 1980, which left behind a vast landscape of ash.

These ash deserts present unique challenges for wildlife. Ash can bury plants and habitats, and fine particulate matter can be harmful to animals breathing that air. However, over time, nature often begins to reassert itself, and new plants can grow, aided by the nutrients from the ashes.

Ash deserts are important to scientists because they offer insight into the environmental impacts of volcanic eruptions. Studying these landscapes can help understand how ecosystems recover after major disturbances. These deserts are testaments to the Earth's ability to transform radically in a short period of time under the influence of geological forces.

Fact 71 - Past Eruptions

Have you ever thought about the history of past volcanic eruptions? Each volcano has its own geological history, marked by periods of activity and rest. Studying past eruptions is essential for understanding the nature of a volcano and predicting its future behavior. Scientists use a variety of methods, such as analysis of ash deposits and volcanic rocks, to reconstruct these events.

These investigations can reveal incredibly powerful eruptions, sometimes much larger than those seen in recent human history. For example, the eruption of the Toba super volcano, about 74,000 years ago, is considered one of the largest of all time, having had a significant impact on the global climate.

In addition to providing information about specific events, the study of past eruptions helps to understand the eruptive cycles of volcanoes. Some volcanoes exhibit recurring patterns of activity, while others show more sporadic and unpredictable behaviors.

Knowledge of past eruptions is therefore crucial for the prevention of volcanic hazards. By understanding how a volcano has behaved in the past, scientists can better assess future risks and help protect communities living nearby. These historical studies are a window into the power and history of our dynamic planet.

Fact 72 - Smoke Signals

Have you ever seen columns of smoke rising from a volcano? These "smoke signals" are often a precursor to increased volcanic activity. They consist of water vapor, gas, and sometimes small amounts of ash. These emissions can vary in intensity and are carefully monitored by volcanologists.

The presence of smoke or steam indicates that the magma is close enough to the surface to heat groundwater, creating steam. The colour and density of the smoke can give clues to the processes taking place beneath the surface. For example, white smoke usually indicates water vapor, while grayer smoke may contain ash or other particles.

Observing and analyzing these smoke signals is crucial for predicting impending eruptions. Changes in the amount and composition of smoke may indicate that magma is moving or pressure is increasing in the volcanic system.

These smoke signals are an important reminder of the need for constant monitoring of active volcanoes. They help scientists assess the risks of eruption and provide timely warnings to local communities. Thus, columns of smoke are not only an impressive natural phenomenon; They are also an essential tool for volcanic risk management.

Fact 73 - Fairy Chimneys

Have you ever seen amazing rock structures called fairy chimneys? These natural formations, often associated with volcanic regions, are columns of rock that stand like towers. They are formed by differential erosion, where softer parts of the rock are eroded faster than harder ones.

These chimneys are usually created in areas where layers of volcanic ash or tuff have been deposited. Over time, erosion caused by wind and water hollows out these deposits, leaving behind more resistant columns of rock. Sometimes a harder stone at the top of the column protects the material underneath, forming a kind of cap.

One of the most famous examples of these formations can be found in Cappadocia, Turkey. This region, rich in history and unique landscapes, has countless fairy chimneys, some of which have even been carved into houses or churches.

Fairy chimneys are not only fascinating for their beauty; They are also windows into the geological history of a region. They reveal the erosive and volcanic processes that have shaped the landscape over millennia. These formations are therefore important natural attractions, offering unique perspectives on the dynamic forces that shape our planet.

Fact 74 - Volcanoes and Oceans

Have you ever thought about the impact of volcanoes on the oceans? Submarine volcanoes and volcanic eruptions play a crucial role in the formation of new seabeds and influence ocean chemistry. These interactions between volcanoes and oceans are fundamental to understanding many aspects of our planet.

The majority of volcanic eruptions occur under the oceans, along mid-ocean ridges. These eruptions create new seafloor rocks, a process called ocean floor expansion. When the lava emitted by these volcanoes cools and solidifies on contact with water, it forms new layers of basaltic rock.

Underwater volcanoes can also influence marine life. The minerals and gases released by these eruptions provide essential nutrients that nourish ocean ecosystems. In some cases, underwater eruptions create hydrothermal vents, providing a unique habitat for various life forms.

Interactions between volcanoes and oceans are also important for regulating the global climate. Volcanic gases such as carbon dioxide can affect the chemical composition of the ocean, influencing the global climate. These processes show the importance of volcanoes in Earth's natural systems, demonstrating their essential role in the formation of our marine and global environment.

Fact 75 - Acid Lakes

Have you ever seen an acidic lake in a volcanic crater? These amazing lakes are formed when water accumulates in a crater and mixes with volcanic gases like sulfur dioxide or hydrogen chloride. This chemical reaction creates strong acids, giving the lake a very low pH, often less than 3, similar to that of vinegar or lemon juice.

These acidic lakes often exhibit vibrant colors, ranging from yellow to emerald green, due to minerals and chemical reactions in the water. Lake Kawah Ijen in Indonesia, for example, is famous for its intense turquoise blue hue, a result of its high acidity and the presence of sulfur.

While these lakes are visually fascinating, they can be extremely dangerous. Their corrosive water can cause severe burns, and the gases emitted are often toxic. It is therefore essential to approach them with caution and under the supervision of experienced guides.

Acid lakes are of great scientific interest. They offer researchers the opportunity to study the interactions between water and volcanic processes, as well as microbial life adapted to these extreme environments. These lakes are striking examples of how geological activities can radically transform landscapes and create unique ecosystems.

Fact 76 - Lava Domes

Have you ever seen a lava dome? Unlike explosive eruptions that produce ash and slag, lava domes form when viscous lava accumulates around the eruptive vent. This type of silica-rich lava cools and hardens quickly, piling the lava in successive layers to form a dome.

These domes can vary in size, with some reaching impressive heights and diameters. Their growth can be slow and steady or occur in rapid flare-ups. A famous example is the lava dome of Mount St. Helens, formed after its 1980 eruption.

Although lava domes are not usually associated with catastrophic eruptions, they can be dangerous. Their unstable surface can collapse, causing lava flows or avalanches of debris. In addition, the pressure built up under a dome can sometimes lead to explosive eruptions.

Lava domes are important for understanding volcanic processes. Their formation offers scientists valuable information about the nature of magma and the underlying conditions that lead to different types of eruptions. Thus, these fascinating structures are windows into the diversity and complexity of volcanic activities.

Fact 77 - Volcanic Avalanches

Have you ever heard of volcanic avalanches? These devastating phenomena, also known as avalanche debris, occur when a large amount of rock material from a volcano collapses and rolls down its slopes at high speed. These avalanches can be triggered by an eruption, an earthquake, or simply by gravity acting on an unstable volcano flank.

A volcanic avalanche can carry a mixture of rock, ash, soil, and even snow or ice, depending on the volcano's environment. This moving mass can travel considerable distances, destroying everything in its path. It can also trigger other dangerous phenomena, such as tsunamis if there is a body of water in its path.

One of the most infamous examples is the Mount St. Helens debris avalanche in 1980. This avalanche was one of the largest ever recorded and drastically altered the surrounding landscape, destroying large areas of forest.

Volcanic avalanches are an important topic of study for geologists and volcanologists. Understanding how and why they occur is crucial to assessing volcanic hazards and implementing preventive measures. These phenomena show the devastating power of volcanoes and the need to monitor and respect these sleeping giants of our planet.

Fact 78 - Volcanic Treasures

Have you ever thought about the treasures that volcanoes hold? Beyond their destructive power, volcanoes are an incredible source of natural wealth. They produce a variety of minerals, rocks, and even gemstones, often sought after for their beauty and scientific value.

Volcanoes are particularly known for their role in the formation of gemstones like diamonds, which form under high pressure in the Earth's mantle and are sometimes brought to the surface by volcanic eruptions. In addition, minerals such as obsidian, a glassy volcanic rock, are prized for their unique appearance and physical properties.

In addition to minerals and gemstones, volcanoes also contribute to the formation of fertile soils. The ash and other material ejected by volcanoes is rich in nutrients that can enrich soils and promote plant growth, which is beneficial for agriculture.

These volcanic treasures are not only economically valuable; They are also important for science. The study of volcanic materials helps geologists better understand the Earth's internal processes and the history of its volcanic activity. Thus, volcanoes are a source of natural wonders, offering a glimpse into the power and bounty of our planet.

Fact 79 - Whims of Magma

Have you ever thought about how magma influences the activity of a volcano? Magma, the molten rock fluid beneath the Earth's surface, plays a crucial role in the behavior of volcanoes. Its composition, temperature, and viscosity determine the type of volcanic eruption.

Magma can vary greatly in its chemical composition. Silica-rich magma (such as rhyolite) is generally more viscous and can lead to explosive eruptions. In contrast, silica-poor magma (such as basalt) is more fluid and often leads to effusive eruptions, with lava flows.

The temperature of the magma is also a key factor. Hotter magma is generally less viscous and can escape more easily from the magma chamber, while colder, more viscous magma can lead to pressure build-up and more violent eruptions.

Scientists study magma to better understand and predict volcanic eruptions. By analyzing eruptive rock samples, they can infer the composition and properties of the magma, which helps determine the potential hazards associated with a volcano.

Thus, the "vagaries of magma" are essential in determining the nature of volcanic eruptions. They show the complexity and variability of the processes that take place beneath the surface of our planet, directly influencing the phenomena we observe on the surface.

Fact 80 - Eruptions at Sea

Have you ever heard of underwater volcanic eruptions? These eruptions occur at the bottom of the oceans and are responsible for the formation of new seabeds. Although they are often less visible than their terrestrial counterparts, submarine eruptions play a crucial role in the Earth's dynamics.

These eruptions most often occur along mid-ocean ridges, where tectonic plates move apart. When this happens, magma rises to fill the gap, creating new ocean rocks. This process is a key component of the expansion of the ocean floor, a phenomenon that contributes to the continuous reshaping of the Earth's surface.

One of the peculiarities of submarine eruptions is the formation of "pillow lavas". These unique structures form when the emitted lava cools rapidly on contact with cold water, creating rounded, cushion-like shapes.

Although submarine eruptions are generally less destructive than land-based eruptions, they can still have a significant impact on the marine environment. The gases and heat emitted can affect local ecosystems, and large eruptions can even generate tsunamis.

Eruptions at sea are therefore a fascinating aspect of our planet's volcanic activity.

Fact 81 - Mountains of Fire

Have you ever been amazed by the majesty of the "mountains of fire", the active volcanoes that seem to burn from the inside out when they erupt? These mountains are spectacles of nature, demonstrating both its beauty and power. When volcanoes erupt, they spew lava, ash, and gases into the atmosphere, creating impressive images.

These eruptions are not only visually spectacular; They also play a crucial role in the geology of our planet. Volcanoes help shape landscapes, create new land, and help recycle the earth's crust. For example, islands formed by volcanic activity, such as Hawaii, are a direct result of these mountains of fire.

Active volcanoes are often revered and feared in local cultures. They are considered powerful entities, capable of creating and destroying. Their activity has inspired many legends and beliefs throughout the centuries.

These mountains of fire are also important subjects of study for scientists. By studying volcanoes, geologists can learn more about the Earth's internal processes and better understand the risks associated with eruptions. Thus, these volcanoes are not just natural wonders; They are also windows into the dynamics of our planet.

Fact 82 - Refuges in the Lava

Have you ever imagined that lava flows could offer natural refuges? After a volcanic eruption subsides and lava hardens, cavities and tunnels can form in the cooled rock. These structures, known as lava tubes or lava tubes, are created when the outer surface of the lava flow cools and hardens while the lava underneath continues to flow.

These lava tubes can become unique ecosystems, home to a variety of plants and animals. In some cases, they provide critical habitat for specific species, providing protection from predators and extreme weather. Lava caves are also places of research for biologists and geologists, offering clues to past volcanic activity and the evolution of isolated ecosystems.

A notable example of these structures can be found in Hawaii Volcanoes National Park, where the Thurston lava tube offers a fascinating glimpse into an underground world formed by volcanic forces.

These lava tunnels and caves are natural wonders that are a testament to nature's ingenuity in creating unique ecosystems. They attract cavers, tourists and researchers, all fascinated by the mysteries hidden in these natural refuges formed by lava.

Fact 83 - Lava Trail

Have you ever followed the path of lava during a volcanic eruption? This path that the lava takes from the crater to its final destination is a fascinating and powerful spectacle of nature. The direction and speed of the lava flow depends on several factors, including the topography of the terrain, the viscosity of the lava, and the slope of the volcano.

Lava can take different forms as it flows. For example, pāhoehoe lava, typical of Hawaiian volcanoes, is relatively fluid and can form smooth, undulating structures. In contrast, ʻaʻā lava is rougher and creates choppy, bumpy surfaces. The way lava moves and cools can also create unique formations, like lava tubes.

Lava flows aren't just visually impressive; They play an important role in the formation of landscapes. They can create new land, alter existing ecosystems, and even create natural barriers. For example, islands formed by lava flows in the ocean can create new habitats for marine wildlife.

The path of the lava is also crucial for volcanological research. By studying how lava moves and cools, scientists can better understand the properties of magma and the internal dynamics of the volcano. Thus, the path taken by lava is not only a remarkable natural phenomenon, but also a valuable source of scientific information.

Fact 84 - Volcanoes and History

Have you ever thought about the impact of volcanoes on human history? Throughout the ages, volcanic eruptions have had a profound effect on civilizations, shaping cultures, altering landscapes, and influencing historical events. These powerful eruptions have often been recorded in legends, myths, and historical chronicles.

For example, the eruption of Mount Vesuvius in 79 A.D. buried the Roman cities of Pompeii and Herculaneum, preserving a moment frozen in time and providing invaluable information about life in Roman times. These cities have become key archaeological sites, offering a unique insight into ancient Roman civilization.

In many cultures, volcanoes have been revered and feared as deities or symbols of power. Their imposing presence and spectacular eruptions have led to their integration into various beliefs and rituals. For example, in Hawaiian mythology, the volcano goddess Pele is worshipped and respected.

Volcanoes have also played a role in more recent events, affecting wars, migrations, and environmental changes. For example, the eruption of Mount Tambora in 1815 resulted in the "year without a summer", with global climate repercussions.

Thus, volcanoes are not only geological features, but also key players in human history.

Fact 85 - Firestorms

Have you ever heard of "firestorms" caused by volcanoes? These spectacular phenomena, although rare, occur during massive eruptions. Firestorms are volcanic thunderstorms created by the intense heat and charged particles emitted during an eruption. These elements interact with the atmosphere to produce lightning, thunder, and sometimes intense rain.

These storms form when the huge columns of ash and gas ejected by the volcano rise into the atmosphere. The friction between the ash particles can generate static electricity, resulting in spectacular flashes of lightning. These lightning strikes are often much more intense than those of normal thunderstorms.

An impressive example of a firestorm was observed during the eruption of the Eyjafjallajökull volcano in Iceland in 2010. Images of the eruption showed bright flashes streaking across the ash plume, creating a spectacle that was both beautiful and threatening.

These firestorms aren't just a stunning natural spectacle; they are also of scientific importance. Studying these phenomena helps researchers better understand the interactions between volcanoes and the atmosphere. Thus, volcanic firestorms are impressive manifestations of the power of volcanoes and their ability to influence the earth's environment.

Fact 86 - Sculpted Landscapes

Have you ever contemplated the way volcanoes sculpt landscapes? Volcanic eruptions, while destructive, play a crucial role in the formation of new landscapes and the modification of existing ones. Lava flows, ejected ash, and even avalanches of volcanic debris help shape the landform of our planet.

Lava flows, for example, can create vast plains or unique rock formations as they cool and solidify. Famous examples include the lava fields of Hawaii, where basaltic lava formed lunar landscapes. Similarly, ash and pyroclastic material emitted during eruptions can cover large areas, changing topography and enriching the soil with minerals.

In some cases, volcanoes contribute to the creation of entire islands. Volcanic islands, such as the Galapagos archipelago, were born from underwater volcanic activity and continue to evolve with each new eruption. These islands provide unique habitats for flora and fauna and are important study areas for scientists.

The landscapes shaped by volcanoes are not only important for their beauty and geological diversity; they are also crucial for understanding the Earth's dynamical processes.

Fact 87 - Thermal Fields

Have you ever explored thermal fields near volcanoes? These areas are characterized by intense geothermal activity, where heat from magma close to the earth's surface heats groundwater. These thermal fields can take the form of hot springs, geysers, fumaroles, and bubbling mud pools.

Thermal fields are often located near active volcanoes or tectonic rift zones. Water heated by magma rises to the surface, loading with minerals along the way. This water can reach high temperatures, creating spectacular phenomena like geysers, which spew hot water and steam into the air.

In addition to their beauty, these thermal fields are of great scientific importance. They offer researchers the opportunity to study geothermal processes and understand how the Earth's thermal energy is transferred to its surface. In addition, organisms that live in these extreme conditions, known as extremophiles, are being studied to understand the limits of life on Earth and, potentially, on other planets.

Thermal fields are also a valuable resource for geothermal energy, a renewable and sustainable energy. By capturing steam and hot water from these fields, it is possible to generate electricity or heat buildings.

Fact 88 - Night Eruptions

Have you ever had the chance to observe a nighttime volcanic eruption? These eruptions are particularly spectacular at night. The glowing lava and the bursts of light created by the explosions offer a striking spectacle against the dark sky. At night, the brightness of the lava and the flames are even more obvious and beautiful, turning the sky into a canvas of vibrant colors.

These nocturnal eruptions are not only a visual spectacle but also an important natural phenomenon. The glowing glow of the lava and the flashes of light produced by the gas explosions provide visual clues to the strength of the eruption and the behavior of the volcano. Photographers and volcanologists often seek to capture these moments for their beauty and scientific value.

Seeing a nighttime eruption can be both mesmerizing and intimidating. It is a reminder of the raw power of nature and the ability of our planet to manifest itself in dramatic ways. These eruptions are reminders of the Earth's active internal dynamics and the immense energy beneath its surface.

These nocturnal eruptions are not only impressive natural phenomena; They are also a warning of the dangers that volcanoes can pose. Communities living near volcanoes should be especially vigilant at night, when signs of an impending eruption may be more visible.

Fact 89 - Ancient Volcanoes

Have you ever explored the remains of ancient volcanoes? These structures, which ceased their eruptive activity millennia ago, are fascinating witnesses to the Earth's geological history. Although these volcanoes no longer pose a threat of eruption, they continue to shape the landscape and offer unique perspectives on past volcanic processes.

Ancient volcanoes, often eroded by time, can come in a variety of shapes, from collapsed craters to eroded cones. These structures can reveal the inner layers of the volcano, offering insight into the different phases of its eruptive activity. For example, extinct volcanoes such as Mount Kilimanjaro in Tanzania or Mount Fuji in Japan, have iconic silhouettes that dominate the landscape.

These ancient giants are important to geologists who study rocks and sediments to understand the volcanic history of an area. They can give clues about the types of magma involved in past eruptions, eruptive cycles, and even regional and global climate change.

In addition to their scientific interest, ancient volcanoes are often sites of cultural and historical significance. They are frequently associated with local legends and play an important role in regional ecosystems, often home to unique biodiversity. These eroded relics are reminders of the power of nature and its lasting impact on our planet.

Fact 90 - Volcanic Sky

Have you ever observed the sky during or after a volcanic eruption? Volcanoes have the ability to transform the sky in dramatic ways. During an eruption, the plume of ash and gas can rise miles into the atmosphere, changing the color and texture of the sky.

During a major eruption, the sky above the volcano can become dark and threatening, filled with ash and particles. This darkness can extend over great distances, sometimes affecting entire regions. In addition, ash and gases in the atmosphere can create sunsets and sunrises of extraordinary color, ranging from deep red to purple.

These atmospheric phenomena are not only visually impressive; They are also of great scientific interest. The ash and gases emitted during an eruption can have an impact on the climate, temporarily cooling the Earth's global temperature. Scientists are studying these effects to better understand the interactions between volcanoes and climate.

The "volcanic sky" is therefore a testament to the impressive strength of volcanoes and their ability to influence our environment in dramatic and profound ways. These changes in the sky can be both a warning of the destructive power of volcanoes and an astonishing demonstration of natural beauty.

Fact 91 - Sleeping Colossi

Have you ever contemplated the dormant volcanoes, those silent colossi that often dominate the landscape with their imposing presence? These volcanoes, currently inactive, have not erupted in centuries or even millennia, but they retain the potential to awaken one day. Their apparent sleep does not mean that they are switched off, but rather in a dormant state.

Dormant volcanoes are important to volcanological science. Their study allows researchers to understand the cycles of volcanic activity over long periods of time. By examining lava and ash deposits, as well as changes in the surrounding topography and geology, scientists can assess the volcano's eruptive history and anticipate its future behavior.

These sleeping giants are not just objects of scientific study; They also play a significant cultural and spiritual role in many regions. Often considered sacred or shrouded in myth and legend, these volcanoes shape the identity and beliefs of the communities that live in their shadow.

Thus, sleeping colossi are fascinating elements of the earth's landscape. They are a reminder of the latent power of the Earth and the possibility of unpredictable future events. Their presence continues to inspire, intrigue, and challenge humans, connecting us to the natural dynamics of our planet.

Fact 92 - Voice of the Volcanoes

Have you ever heard the "voices" of volcanoes? This poetic term refers to the sounds produced by active volcanoes. These sounds, which can range from a dull rumble to deafening explosions, are the result of various geological processes at work beneath the Earth's surface.

Volcanoes make sounds for a variety of reasons. For example, rumblings can be caused by the movement of magma and gases inside the volcano. Explosions, on the other hand, occur when the pressure of accumulated gases is released abruptly. These sounds aren't just an auditory show; They are also key indicators of volcanic activity.

Scientists use special instruments, such as seismographs, to record and analyze these sounds. By studying the "voices" of volcanoes, they can gather valuable information about magma movements and pressure levels, helping to predict potential eruptions.

Thus, the "voices" of volcanoes are more than just a natural curiosity. They are a window into the complex internal processes of volcanoes and an essential tool for monitoring and predicting eruptions. These sounds remind us that volcanoes are dynamic, active, and often unpredictable entities.

Fact 93 - Isles of Fire

Have you ever visited or dreamed of visiting an "island of fire", an island formed entirely by volcanic activity? These islands were born from the depths of the sea thanks to underwater volcanic eruptions. As the eruptions progress, lava and ash accumulate until they emerge from the ocean, forming new land.

The volcanic islands offer unique and varied landscapes, ranging from black sand beaches formed by volcanic ash to majestic craters and mountain peaks. Famous examples include the Hawaiian Islands, Iceland, and the Galapagos Islands, each with its own natural beauty and outstanding biodiversity.

These islands are not only attractive tourist destinations; They are also of great scientific importance. Researchers study these islands to understand the formation of volcanoes, the evolution of island ecosystems, and the impact of eruptions on the marine environment.

The "islands of fire" are also crucial habitats for many unique species. The isolation and peculiar environmental conditions have led to remarkable biodiversity, with many endemic species that are found nowhere else on the planet.

Thus, the islands formed by volcanoes are natural wonders that capture our imagination.

Fact 94 - Magic Mountains

Have you ever felt the magic of gazing at a volcanic mountain? These "magic mountains" are not just geological wonders; They are also shrouded in mystery, legends and deep cultural meanings. Volcanoes, with their imposing shape and destructive and creative power, have often been seen as sacred places or portals to other worlds in various cultures.

The presence of a volcano can influence an entire region, not only through its geological impact, but also through its cultural and spiritual influence. For example, Mount Fuji in Japan and Popocatépetl in Mexico are shrouded in myth and respect, embodying the beauty and power of nature in the collective consciousness.

These mountains are also unique ecosystems. Their nutrient-rich soil, from past eruptions, allows for remarkable biological diversity. Many species of plants and animals find refuge on their slopes, some of which do not exist anywhere else.

In addition, the "magic mountains" are valuable places of study for scientists. They offer information on past and current volcanic activity, helping to understand the underlying geological processes and potential risks to surrounding populations.

Fact 95 - Volcanoes Visible from Space

Have you ever imagined seeing a volcano from space? Some volcanoes are so huge and their eruptions so powerful that they are visible from Earth's orbit. These "volcanoes visible from space" provide spectacular images and help scientists study volcanic phenomena on a planetary scale.

Satellite images of volcanoes offer a unique view of eruptions, ash plumes, and lava flows. For example, the eruptions of Mount Etna in Sicily and Kīlauea in Hawaii were captured from space, showing the impressive scale of their activity. These images help assess the impact of eruptions on the atmosphere and environment.

Satellites play a crucial role in monitoring volcanoes, especially in remote or hard-to-reach areas. They allow for continuous observation and can detect early signs of an eruption, such as temperature changes or ground deformations.

Volcanoes visible from space are therefore important subjects of study for modern volcanology. They help researchers better understand volcanic dynamics and improve monitoring and risk prevention systems. These views from space remind us of how interconnected and visible our planet's natural phenomena are on a global scale.

Fact 96 - Secrets of the Magma

Have you ever thought about the secrets hidden in magma, the molten rock beneath the Earth's surface? Magma is the engine of volcanoes, and its composition, temperature, and viscosity play a key role in the type and strength of a volcanic eruption. Understanding magma is key to unraveling the mysteries of volcanoes.

The composition of magma varies according to the chemical elements it contains. Silica-rich magma, for example, is more viscous and can lead to explosive eruptions, while silica-poor magma is more fluid and promotes effusive eruptions. These differences influence how lava moves and cools, shaping the surrounding landscape.

The temperature of the magma is also crucial. Hotter magma can contain more dissolved gas, increasing the likelihood of explosive eruptions. By studying these properties, scientists can better predict the behaviors of volcanoes and the associated risks.

The secrets of magma are not only relevant to the prediction of eruptions. They are also essential for understanding the formation and evolution of the Earth's crust. Movements of magma beneath the surface can form new mountains, reshape continents, and influence tectonic activity.

Fact 97 - Volcanoes and Legends

Have you ever heard the legends and myths surrounding volcanoes? Throughout history and in different cultures, volcanoes have often been shrouded in mysteries and fascinating tales. These legends reflect the way humans have attempted to understand and explain volcanic phenomena, often perceived as manifestations of the gods or supernatural forces.

In many cultures, volcanoes are seen as abodes of deities or portals to underworlds. For example, in Hawaiian mythology, Pele is the goddess of fire and volcanoes, often associated with the volcano Kīlauea. His stories depict his power and temperamental nature, symbolizing the unpredictable nature of volcanoes.

These mythological tales are not mere tales; They play an important role in cultural understanding and respect for natural forces. They offer insights into how ancient peoples interpreted natural events and incorporated them into their worldview.

Today, these legends continue to fascinate and inspire. They connect us to our past and enrich our appreciation of natural phenomena. Volcanoes, as subjects of these legends, are not just geological features; They are also powerful symbols in the human imagination, representing creation, destruction, and renewal.

Fact 98 - Light of Lava

Have you ever been amazed by the light emitted by the lava of an erupting volcano? This glowing glow, visible from afar, is a hypnotic and powerful sight. The light from the lava comes from the high temperature of the magma that rises to the surface of the volcano, illuminating the night with its fiery glow.

This light is not only a striking visual spectacle; It is also an indicator of volcanic activity. The color and intensity of the light can vary depending on the temperature of the lava and its composition. For example, iron-rich lava may appear a darker red, while lava with less iron may glow a bright reddish-orange.

Photographers and observers around the world are often captivated by this phenomenon. The images of lava lighting up the night sky or pouring into the ocean, creating luminous clouds of steam, are spectacular and a reminder of the power of nature.

Lava lumen is also an important subject of study for volcanologists. By observing these lights, scientists can gather valuable information about the temperature of the lava, the characteristics of the eruption, and the internal dynamics of the volcano.

Fact 99 - Volcanic Heroes

Have you ever heard of volcanic heroes? This term refers to people who, in the face of the dangers of volcanoes, take risks to study, monitor, and protect others from potential threats. These heroes include volcanologists, rescue workers, and even locals who have played crucial roles in eruptions.

Volcanologists, in particular, are often on the front lines, approaching active volcanoes to gather vital data. Their work is essential to understand the mechanisms of eruptions and to develop forecasting and warning systems. Their research is helping to save lives by providing crucial information about impending eruptions.

In addition to scientists, heroes from local communities also play an important role. These people often help with evacuation and awareness of volcanic hazards, sometimes putting their own lives on the line to help others. Their knowledge of the terrain and local culture is invaluable in an emergency.

These volcanic heroes are not only figures of bravery; They embody the union of science, compassion and courage. Their dedication to studying these mountains of fire and protecting the surrounding communities is a reminder of the strength of the human spirit in the face of the powerful forces of nature.

Fact 100 - Volcanic Visions

Have you ever been captivated by volcanic visions, those spectacular and powerful images of volcanoes in action? These scenes, ranging from glowing lava flows to eruptions exploding in the sky, offer glimpses of the brute force and beauty of nature. Volcanic visions aren't just natural spectacles; they are also reminders of the dynamics and power of the Earth.

Photographers and filmmakers around the world seek to capture these awe-inspiring moments, often at the risk of their own safety. These images can be both terrifying and beautiful, showing glowing lava making its way across the landscape, or columns of ash and gas rising to the heavens.

These visions are not only aesthetically striking; They are also valuable for awareness and education. By sharing these images, the media and scientists can raise awareness about the power of volcanoes and the risks they pose. These images can also inspire a sense of respect and wonder for our planet's natural processes.

Thus, "volcanic visions" combine beauty, science, and adventure. They capture the imagination and stimulate curiosity, reminding us that, despite advances in technology, we remain at the mercy of our planet's natural forces. These spectacular images are a testament to the ongoing interaction between Earth and its inhabitants, offering windows into a world that is both beautiful and unforgiving.

Conclusion

There you have it, our journey through the fascinating world of volcanoes is coming to an end. I hope you were as captivated by these giants of nature as I was in sharing these stories with you. Through these 100 amazing facts, you have discovered the power and beauty of volcanoes, but also their importance in the formation of our planet and the life it supports.

You've learned how volcanoes can create islands, influence the climate, and even give rise to unique ecosystems. You've explored amazing phenomena like fire cascades, acid crater lakes, and underwater eruptions. But, more importantly, I hope you've understood that, despite their destructive potential, volcanoes play a vital role in the balance of our Earth.

Volcanoes remind us that our planet is alive, dynamic, and constantly evolving. They teach us humility in the face of the forces of nature and the importance of respecting and protecting our environment.

So, keep exploring, asking questions, and looking for answers. The world of volcanoes, just like the rest of our planet, is filled with mysteries to solve and lessons to learn. Keep that thirst for knowledge and wonder for the natural world, and who knows what other incredible adventures await you!

Marc Dresgui

Quiz

1) What is the origin of the Barringer Crater in Arizona, USA?

    a) A massive volcanic eruption.

    b) The impact of an iron and nickel meteorite.

    c) A natural subterranean collapse.

    d) An explosion caused by human activity.

2) How were the Hawaiian Islands formed?

    a) By the accumulation of sediments carried by rivers.

    b) Following a large underwater earthquake.

    c) By underwater volcanic eruptions.

    d) Due to rising sea levels.

3) What was one of the loudest volcanic eruptions ever recorded, the sound of which was heard thousands of miles away?

    a) The eruption of Mount St. Helens in 1980.

    b) The eruption of Krakatoa in 1883.

    c) The eruption of Mount Vesuvius in 79 A.D.

    d) The eruption of Mauna Loa in 1984.

4) What is special about mud volcanoes compared to traditional volcanoes?

    a) They emit toxic ash.

b) They expel extremely hot lava.

c) They spew mud instead of lava.

d) They are exclusively underwater.

5) Where can we observe the natural phenomenon of fire cascades, where lava looks like a liquid waterfall?

a) In Yellowstone National Park, USA.

b) At Mount Fuji, Japan.

c) At Hawaii Volcanoes National Park.

d) At Tongariro National Park, New Zealand.

6) What is the main effect of sulfur dioxide emitted during volcanic eruptions on the Earth's climate?

a) It increases the temperature of the Earth's surface.

b) It forms sulfate aerosols that reflect sunlight, resulting in cooling.

c) It contributes directly to the increase in global precipitation.

d) It increases the greenhouse effect and global warming.

7) What is the main characteristic of extinct volcanoes?

a) They are dormant but can wake up.

b) They erupt at regular intervals.

c) They should never erupt again.

d) They are constantly emitting smoke and gases.

8) What is the main effect of volcanic ash on soils?

a) They always increase the toxicity of the soil.
b) They improve soil fertility thanks to their mineral richness.
c) They make the soil perpetually sterile.
d) They do not change the chemical composition of the soil.

9) What is the main trigger for gas explosions in volcanoes?

a) The accumulation of extreme heat in the crater of the volcano.
b) Tectonic movements beneath the volcano.
c) The sudden release of high-pressure gases trapped in the magma.
d) The infiltration of seawater into the magma chamber.

10) What is a unique feature of wildlife living in volcanic ecosystems?

a) They are all very small in size due to the harsh conditions.
b) They can survive without water for years.

c) They have developed special adaptations to thrive in an environment influenced by volcanic activity.
d) They are all nocturnal species due to the intense daytime heat.

11) What was the major impact of the eruptions of the Siberian Traps about 250 million years ago?

a) They created the first islands in the Pacific Ocean.
b) They contributed to one of the largest mass extinctions in Earth's history.
c) They formed the first mountain ranges.
d) They caused the first ice age on Earth.

12) What is the origin of Crater Lake in Oregon, USA?

a) A massive meteorite impact.
b) An ancient glacier that has melted.
c) A man-made dam.
d) The collapse of a volcano, forming a crater lake.

13) What is a distinguishing feature of super volcanoes compared to regular volcanoes?

a) They are always located underwater.
b) They eject huge amounts of magma during eruptions.
c) They erupt at very regular intervals.
d) They do not produce volcanic ash.

14) What is the main characteristic of an ash desert?

a) A field covered in eternal snow.
b) A landscape formed by the accumulation of large amounts of volcanic ash.
c) A desert environment caused by extreme drought.
d) An area where vegetation is abundant and lush.

15) What is the main characteristic of acid lakes in volcanic craters?

a) They are extremely hot, with temperatures similar to lava.
b) They have a very low pH, often less than 3, due to the presence of volcanic gases.
c) They are usually populated by many species of fish.
d) They are mainly fed by fresh water sources.

16) Where do submarine volcanic eruptions mainly occur?

a) In freshwater lakes and reservoirs.
b) Close to coasts and beaches.
c) Along mid-ocean ridges, where tectonic plates move apart.
d) Beneath icebergs and polar glaciers.

17) What is the main characteristic of "firestorms" during volcanic eruptions?

    a) The formation of fire tornadoes near the volcano.

    b) The appearance of lava tsunamis.

    c) The creation of ash clouds that completely block sunlight.

    d) The production of lightning and thunder due to intense heat and charged particles.

18) What effect can volcanic eruptions have on the sky?

    a) They create the Northern Lights that can be seen all over the world.

    b) They increase the brightness of the sky, making the stars more visible.

    c) They can change the color and texture of the sky, sometimes creating extraordinary sunsets and sunrises.

    d) They cause clouds in the shape of animals and other figures to form.

19) What aspect of volcanoes allows them to be observed from space?

    a) The light emitted by molten lava.

    b) The immense size and powerful eruptions that produce large plumes of ash and lava.

c) The sound of eruptions, detectable by space instruments.
d) The heat emitted by the volcano, visible only at night.

20) What makes "volcanic visions" unique and important?

a) Their ability to accurately predict the next eruption of a volcano.
b) The calming and meditative effect they have on the viewers.
c) Their combination of beauty, scientific significance, and adventure, raising awareness of volcanoes.
d) Their use as the main source of renewable energy.

Answers

1) What is the origin of the Barringer Crater in Arizona, USA?

Correct answer: b) The impact of an iron and nickel meteorite.

2) How were the Hawaiian Islands formed?

Correct answer: (c) By submarine volcanic eruptions.

3) What was one of the loudest volcanic eruptions ever recorded, the sound of which was heard thousands of miles away?

Correct answer: b) The eruption of Krakatoa in 1883.

4) What is special about mud volcanoes compared to traditional volcanoes?

Correct answer: c) They spew mud instead of lava.

5) Where can we observe the natural phenomenon of fire cascades, where lava looks like a liquid waterfall?

Correct answer: c) Hawaii Volcanoes National Park.

6) What is the main effect of sulfur dioxide emitted during volcanic eruptions on the Earth's climate?

Correct answer: b)It forms sulfate aerosols that reflect sunlight, resulting in cooling.

7) What is the main characteristic of extinct volcanoes?

Correct answer: c) They should never erupt again.

8) What is the main effect of volcanic ash on soils?

Correct answer: b)They improve soil fertility due to their mineral content.

9) What is the main trigger for gas explosions in volcanoes?

Correct answer: c) The sudden release of high-pressure gases trapped in the magma.

10) What is a unique feature of wildlife living in volcanic ecosystems?

Correct answer: c) They have developed special adaptations to thrive in an environment influenced by volcanic activity.

11) What was the major impact of the eruptions of the Siberian Traps about 250 million years ago?

Correct answer: b) They contributed to one of the largest mass extinctions in Earth's history.

12) What is the origin of Crater Lake in Oregon, USA?

Correct answer: d) The collapse of a volcano, forming a crater lake.

13) What is a distinguishing feature of super volcanoes compared to regular volcanoes?

Correct answer: b) They eject huge amounts of magma during eruptions.

14) What is the main characteristic of an ash desert?

Correct answer: b) A landscape formed by the accumulation of large amounts of volcanic ash.

15) What is the main characteristic of acid lakes in volcanic craters?

Correct answer: b) They have a very low pH, often less than 3, due to the presence of volcanic gases.

16) Where do submarine volcanic eruptions mainly occur?

Correct answer: c)Along mid-ocean ridges, where tectonic plates move apart.

17) What is the main characteristic of "firestorms" during volcanic eruptions?

Correct answer: (d) The production of lightning and thunder due to intense heat and charged particles.

18) What effect can volcanic eruptions have on the sky?

Correct answer: c) They can change the color and texture of the sky, sometimes creating extraordinary sunsets and sunrises.

19) What aspect of volcanoes allows them to be observed from space?

Correct answer: b) The immense size and powerful eruptions that produce large plumes of ash and lava.

20) What makes "volcanic visions" unique and important?

Correct answer: c) Their combination of beauty, scientific significance, and adventure, raising public awareness of volcanoes.

Manufactured by Amazon.ca
Acheson, AB

13353108R00068